Lampshade Making

-Books 1 and 2-

by

F. J. Christopher

Copyright © 2011 Read Books Ltd.
This book is copyright and may not be
reproduced or copied in any way without
the express permission of the publisher in writing

British Library Cataloguing-in-Publication Data
A catalogue record for this book is available from
the British Library

LAMPSHADE MAKING

BY

F. J. CHRISTOPHER F.R.S.A.

Member: The Guild of Craftworkers
Associate: The Institute of Handicraft Teachers
Editor : *Craftworker* Magazine

CONTENTS

	Page
Preface	9
Introduction	11

Skill in craftsmanship — modern trends — suitability of purpose — sizes and shapes — illuminating suitability — electric light bulbs — suitability of covering materials — colours — fluorescent lighting — initial cost of equipment — materials — principles — decoration — progressive practise.

Chapter I 15

Materials — foundation materials — coverings — decorations — lampshade frames, types and sizes — points to watch when purchasing frames — gimbal fittings to foundation frames — coverings — types — **"Crinothene,"** an ideal material — marking, cutting and jointing — Acetate — handling — fabrics — suitable types — papers — parchment — other covering materials — combinations — Braid — Gimp — Gandyke Braid — Russia Braid — silk cord — fringe — thongings — bindings. **Preparation :** Binding foundation frames — overlapping and finishing. **Pattern making :** Care in making — basic Empire patterns — instructions and diagram. **Patterns for panelled lampshades :** Marking and cutting — preliminary stages.

Chapter II 26

Simple Lampshades — small frames — " butterfly " fitting — inspection — preparation — binding the frame — pattern making — economy in cutting materials — marking parchment — punching thonging holes — thonging the cover — sequence — finishing — lampshade with curved sides — preparation, pattern making, marking out and cutting — stitching the cover — how to stitch **" Crinothene "** — attaching gimp and fringes — a thonged and stitched cover — swivel gimbal — pattern making for an Empire frame — joining the vertical edge — finishing — progress in sequence.

CONTENTS —*cont.*

Page

Chapter III 35
    Flared and fluted lampshade covers: Use of Buckram and Acetate — a flared buckram cover — two-piece frame — preparation — making the cover — simple table for determining dimensions of flared covers — marking out and cutting — assembling — sequence and finishing — variations — other materials. Buckram and fabric — new covers and re-covering — patterns — marking the buckram — joining the materials — cutting to shape — attaching and finishing. A fluted acetate cover — testing for inflammability — foundation frame — gate-legged gimbal — flute patterns — determining dimensions — simple table — guide to flute sizes — alternative method — marking and cutting out — joining the flutes — fitting the cover to the frame — finishing.

Chapter IV 45
    " Crinothene " Covered Lampshades: Possibilities of the material — heat-sealing — strength of the joint — vertical joins — tools to use — testing, practise and method — overlapping — surface modelling. **A double cover:** Use of two colours — foundation frame — gimbal adaptor — interlocking shaped pieces — preparation — pattern making — duplicate testing pattern — assembling and tacking the cover — attaching the cover to the frame — alternative edge shapes. **Fitting Curved Panels:** Suitable frame — checking and preparation — pattern making — marking out and cutting — method of ensuring accurate fitting — frame distortion — common faults — decorating and finishing.

Chapter V 54
    Fabric-covered Lampshades: Methods and application. A simple lampshade — concave panels — inspection and preparation — binding materials — absence of patterns — ensuring material worked on the bias — use of pins — positioning of pins — stretching the material — covering half the frame — trimming, stitching and finishing — fitted linings. Another method — more difficult frame shape — preparation — fitting separate panels — care in stretching and pinning — sequence of pinning — even tension — stitching, finishing and decorating. A satin-covered standard lampshade — large frame — inspecting and preparing — illustration of points of instruction — different styles of treatment — separate assembly — covering the frame — fitting the lining — pinning, smoothing, trimming and stitching — importance of neatness — shaping the outer cover — marking, cutting and assembling — fitting and fastening the cover — lower panels — decoration and finishing — prowess of the home worker.

CONTENTS—*cont.*

Page

Chapter VI 65
    A Parchment and Velvet Cover: Simple foundation frame — cleaning real Parchment — removing wrinkles and creases — care in handling — preparing the frame — attaching the velvet corner pieces — pinning, trimming and sewing — marking and cutting the parchment panels — attaching the panels — braiding and finishing. **A shade for a Bed Lamp:** Avoidance of a common fault — enclosed tops — preparation — using odd pieces of material — patterns — two-colour cover — attaching the acetate — decorating and finishing. **Empire shade with modelled edge:** Suitable frame — **" Barbola "** edges — assembling the cover — testing for fit — overlapping ends — joining the vertical seam — fitting the cover — attachment to the frame — the **" Barbola "** edge — depth — working the material — attaching, modelling and finishing.

Chapter VII 75
    Different treatment of materials — a craft of invention — use of two materials — novel form of decoration — preparation — pattern making — cutting thonging holes — decorating the inner cover — assembling the cover — variation of decoration. **A stencil-cut Parchment Cover:** Preparation and shaping the cover — 'ties' in cutting designs — cutting the designs — glueing the vertical joins — attaching the two-part cover — variety in treatment. **A Novelty frameless lampshade:** Ingenious treatment — strip cover — heat-sealing ends and edges — washer reinforcement — fitting to a base. **" Crinothene " covers for tube lighting:** Frames — construction — future developments. **Cylindrical Lampshade:** Dimensions — wood base — batten-holder — pattern and cutting — assembling — finishing. **A Nursery Lampshade:** Rotating inside cover — gimbal adaptor — details of construction — metal top piece — assembling the rotating cover — fitting and adjustment.

Chapter VIII 87
    Lampshade bases: Aid to sales — use of common articles and objects — converting a vase — plug for the neck — suitable materials — shaping the plug — care in fitting — attaching the socket — another pottery base — different conversion treatment — use of back plates — drilling pottery and glass — suitable lubricant — practise — assembling the lamp base. A covered bottle — pattern — use of **" Crinothene "** — thonged corners — finishing — assembling — light reflection. A preserve jar with moulded cover — use of **" Wallart "** — mixing and applying — drying — final coat — stippled finish — insulating the flex hole. A candle-

CONTENTS—cont.

stick lamp base made from "**Crinothene**" — fittings — making the column — heat-sealed edges — making the base — handle — wiring-up and fitting — a cord-covered base — suitable foundation — attaching the cord — decorative treatment.

Chapter IX 98

Decorating Lampshades: Suitable materials — applications — velvet — Ruching — description — stitching — drawing up — fastening off — Shell Ruching — diagonal stitching — finishing — Double Ruching — puffed ruching — Two-Colour Ruching — use of two ribbons — method — finishing. **Parchment:** Crackled 'antique' Parchment — imitation crackle effect — use of chemicals — small pattern — smoothing ridges — darkening cracks — finishing — practise — better method — necessity of plenty of practise — glue solution — applying the solution — liability to cockle — cracking in shrink-drying — avoidance of small pattern — darkening the cracks — finishing — emphasis on practise. **Painting on Parchment:** Suitable mediums — tracing the decorative design — degreasing the decoration area — changing colour values — fading of colours — use of transparent colours. **Decorative Thonging:** Suggestions — suitable leatherwork thonging stitches — silk cords. **Other Materials:** Use of lace — labels and stamps — a calendar lampshade cover — suitable Christmas gift — use of artificial flowers — "**Saree Relief Colours**" and metallic powders — applique — possibilities of the craft — assistance in obtaining supplies.

PREFACE

THE craft of Lampshade Making is one that has much to recommend it; the work is clean and pleasant—no very great outlay is necessary to commence with, and there is a very good market for the finished products provided they are well made and reasonably priced. This book presents the beginner with the knowledge to begin this profitable and interesting home craft.

Lampshade making is a craft. Although it cannot be regarded as one of the traditional or basic crafts, such as Handweaving, Leatherwork, Basketry or Pottery, it is a craft —a modern craft. In recent years, many new materials have been produced, which are suitable for covering lampshades; there has been progress in design, and the technique of construction has advanced. To-day, lampshade making is a skilled craft, and whatever the purpose of the lampshade maker—be it to make a few lampshades for the home, or production in quantity as a commercial venture—skill is needed to manipulate the materials in making the product a worthwhile contribution to modern craftsmanship.

As with any other handicraft, perfection can only be attained by patient practise of acquired knowledge—there are no short cuts—*Lampshade Making* sets out to provide that knowledge.

Bournemouth,   F.J.C.
1950.

INTRODUCTION

Skill in craftsmanship — modern trends — suitability of purpose — sizes and shapes — illuminating suitability — electric light bulbs — suitability of covering materials — colours — fluorescent lighting — initial cost of equipment — materials — principles — decoration — progressive practise.

IN my Preface I described lampshade making as a skilled craft, though I have no doubt that many people will disagree with me. It appears very easy to cover a wire frame with material, fasten it to the frame and apply some form of decoration, but those of my readers who have attempted making or re-covering lampshades, and those who have had some experience in the craft will agree with me that there is more in lampshade making than the mere cutting, shaping and fixing of materials. The wide variety of suitable covering materials—soft fabrics, parchment and papers, plastics and other materials—and the modern trend of simplicity in design, coupled with suitability of purpose, necessitate careful consideration in application and construction. It is not merely sufficient to make a shade for a lamp (this could easily be accomplished by wrapping a sheet of newspaper round it), but to make a lampshade that will be suitable in every way for the purpose of its use, and for the setting in which it is to be placed.

The most obvious consideration is size. Very few people would fit a small candle-shade to a floor-standard, but many disregard the consideration of size for purpose when making pendant lampshades, shades for passage and hall lamps, bedside lamps and table lamps. The size of the lampshade should be carefully considered in relation to the size, and sometimes the shape, of the room in which it is to be used.

The shape of the lamp is important also. It should be remembered that not always the best light is obtained from a lamp with an open-based shade. Sometimes a better light is obtained by using a shade with a closed base, and with an open top so that the light is reflected from a ceiling—it depends on how near the lamp is to the ceiling. The lampshade for a reading lamp should be capable of directing the light where it is most wanted. Lampshades used in halls and passages should be so constructed as to do their job efficiently, and that is true also of lampshades fitted to lights in dining rooms, living rooms and bedrooms. Where the maximum amount of light is required the shade should be the most suitable size and shape.

Not always are dull dingy lights due to the shape of the lampshade. Very often the fault is in using an electric lamp bulb of the wrong power. It does not necessarily follow that only low powered lamp bulbs create dull lights. Sometimes the fault is due to using a too highly-powered lamp bulb with the result that the covering material becomes scorched. A simple example is when a highly-powered lamp bulb is used with a shade covered with oiled paper. The heat generated from the lamp gradually turns the paper brown, and usually the change is so gradual that it is unnoticed; resulting in a shade that restricts light to one part of the room and throws the rest in shadow.

Suitability of purpose is a most important consideration when selecting the types of covering materials for lampshades. Some materials restrict light—others diffuse light. Parchment papers, for example, unless they are of very good quality tend to restrict the illuminating powers of a lamp, while " Crinothene "—a plastic material manufactured specially for covering lampshades—is not at all restrictive and will permit and assist the diffusion of a soft clear light. These are general examples only. There are many variations in degree, and the simplest method of determining the light restriction or suffusion power of any particular material, is to test it over a naked light bulb.

Colours also play a most important part in suitability of purpose, and these too should be tested, both in natural and in artificial light. Some coloured materials change their colour values in different lights. The colour of a lampshade cover, if the shade is to be used in a particular room, should tone with the existing colour scheme. It should not be unduly obtrusive by day or by night. The type of covering material selected should be consistent with the size of the frame. A heavy bulky material would look completely out of place over a small light frame, and a thin material would be equally out of place on a large heavy frame.

It has been said that making lampshades for covering ordinary electric light bulbs may become obsolete because of the advent of fluorescent lighting, but it will be many, many years before fluorescent lighting supersedes contemporary forms of lighting and, in any case, fluorescent lighting tubes are usually improved by covering them with shades.

The initial cost of equipment for the beginner in lampshade making is not very great. A good sharp pair of scissors is required, and if many shades are to be made, two pairs of scissors will be found very useful; one, a small pair for trimming corners and fine cutting and the other a large pair for cutting heavy materials to shape. A razor blade will be found generally useful, and a small pair of pliers has many uses in the craft. Needles, pins, silks and cottons will be required as the work progresses, and a holing-punch, as used in leatherwork, is necessary when making thonged lampshades. Although thonged lampshades are described in this book, the emphasis is on stitched lampshade covers.

The main materials required are wire foundation frames, covering materials, fastening materials (for joining covers to frames), and decorating and finishing materials. These are described in detail later in the book. None of the materials is very costly in relation to the price of present-day lampshades.

The principles of lampshade making are simple. A wire frame of suitable size and shape is used for the foundation of the lampshade. The frame is covered with material, carefully cut to shape and stitched or thonged to the foundation frame, and the lampshade is finally decorated. Careful consideration should be given to decoration. It is a common fault of beginners—in any craft—to over-embellish the work with surplus decoration, thus detracting from the appearance of the product, wasting time in finishing, and decreasing the value of the work. The lampshade maker who is working for profit should avoid costly and wasteful decoration of his products. Generally, it will be found that most covering materials are sufficiently decorative in themselves, and trimmings used to cover seams and stitches are all that are necessary to finalise the decorative finish.

The value of any particular form of decoration is a matter for individual consideration, as also is the quality of design. What appeals to one person may not suit another, but generally, clean lines, graceful shapes and the avoidance of over-elaborate decoration should be carefully considered when the products are being made for sale.

In lampshade making, as in any other craft, every stage of the work should be carefully carried out. Bad workmanship in the preliminary stages will inevitably show in the finished product. The beginner should commence making simple lampshades, becoming familiar with every part of the work, before attempting the manufacture of shades requiring the use of expensive materials.

A sensible approach to the craft from the very beginning will ensure satisfaction in accomplishment, and provide profit in pleasure.

CHAPTER I

Materials — foundation materials — coverings — decorations — lampshade frames, types and sizes — points to watch when purchasing frames — gimbal fittings to foundation frames — coverings — types — "**Crinothene,**" an ideal material — marking, cutting and jointing — Acetate — handling — fabrics — suitable types — papers — parchment — other materials — combinations — Braid — Gimp — Vandyke Braid — Russia Braid — silk cord — fringe — thongings — bindings. **Preparation:** Binding foundation frames — overlapping and finishing. **Pattern making:** Care in making — basic Empire patterns — instructions and diagram. **Patterns for panelled lampshades:** Marking and cutting — preliminary stages.

THIS chapter deals more fully with the materials mentioned in the introduction. Broadly, materials can be classified under three main headings: Foundations (frames, gimbals and frame attachments), Coverings (the materials used for covering the foundation frames which include bindings for the frames) and Decorations (such as braids, gimps, fringes, etc., for stitched frames, and the materials used for painting and otherwise decorating).

FOUNDATIONS.

The most important materials are the foundation materials —mainly frames. Lampshade frames are mostly made of mild steel wire which is galvanised, some frames are made from brass or copper wire. The lampshade foundation frames are obtainable in a very wide selection range of size and shape, from the very small frames used for making candle shades and bed-lamp shades to large frames for shades for standard lamps and some pendant lamps. Different thicknesses of wire are (or should be) used for making the different sizes of frames. When purchasing frames, make certain that wire of a suitable thickness in relation to the size of the frame, has been used. That is; thin wire for small frames, and thick wire for large frames. This seems so obvious as to be hardly worth mentioning, but it may be found that some careless manufacturers are not particular about using wire of the most suitable thickness for the size of frame. The wire should be thick enough and strong enough to support the frame rigidly and withstand the strain of fixing the covering material.

Most lampshade frames are welded, some are soldered, and when purchasing frames the joints should be carefully inspected to see that they are strong and are not fractured. The wires should not be bent, and the frames should be well shaped. Place the frame on a floor and view it from above. If there is any distortion, you should be able to see it. Distorted frames will not make good lampshades. After viewing the frame from above, hold it at arm's length and ensure that the horizontal wires are level. Make certain that your foundation is a good one. Too often a badly made lampshade is due to a faulty frame.

Most frames are made by hand on shaped blocks and there is bound to be some slight difference in the sizes of panels; that is almost unavoidable, and will not make any very great difference to the lampshade providing the difference is not unduly great. Lampshade foundation frames are obtainable from local Arts & Crafts shops and from mail-order suppliers who specialise in supplying the home craftworker. Most of the frames supplied by different stockists are similar in shape and design, and many stockists will make frames to special shapes and sizes required.

Although frames are not very difficult to make (their manufacture is fully explained in my first book—" How to make Lampshades "), it will usually be found more economical—in time, at least—to purchase ready-made foundation frames.

Frames are made for use with various types of lamps. A pendant lampshade is fitted with a gimbal ring at the top (the gimbal ring is that part of the foundation frame which fits over the lamp-holder socket, and is kept in place on the socket by means of a threaded ring). Frames for table lamps and bedside lamps are fitted with a swivel gimbal which is soldered to the frame. Standard lamp frames are fitted with a large ring which fits over a 'gate-leg' gimbal which in turn is fitted to the lamp-holder socket at the top of the floor standard. The various types of gimbals and fittings are shown in the instructional illustrations, as also are some of the different foundation frame shapes and designs.

COVERINGS

There are several types of covering materials which, broadly speaking, can be classified under three main headings:

Plastics, Fabrics and Papers. Of course, there are other materials suitable for covering lampshades and generally any material which is not completely opaque can be used.

Plastics and Fabrics are the most popular types of covering materials. Papers (including parchment papers, vellum and coloured cartridge papers, oiled papers, etc.), are not widely used in present-day lampshade making. A description of the materials is given below, also brief notes on marking the materials and cutting them.

" Crinothene " (**Plastic**): This is a product of **Imperial Chemical Industries Ltd.** It is a tough flexible material which is produced in a wide range of attractive colours. Very light in weight, it is extremely durable and, unlike many other lampshade materials will not, under normal conditions, become brittle with age, or be affected by the heat generated by an electric light bulb. " Crinothene " is not more inflammable than wood, does not trap dust, and is easily cleaned by washing with warm soapy water. This tough plastic material[1], has an attractive roughly-patterned surface not unlike that of crêpe rubber. " Crinothene " is extremely pleasing in appearance when covering a lighted lamp, and when viewed by natural light. The light scattering properties of its roughened surface provide a glare-less clear-light diffusion.

" Crinothene " is easy to work. It can be cut with a sharp knife, scissors or razor blade and can be jointed by stitching, with thonging, or by heat-sealing with a soldering iron. It can be marked with chalk. It is strong enough to maintain lampshade rigidity when used for covering frames without side members. It may be painted but, usually, it will be found sufficiently decorative in itself.

Manufactured especially for covering lampshades, " **Crinothene** " is, without doubt, the best of the plastic materials. It may also be used in craftwork for making handbags and belts, table mats, blotter covers, firescreens and many other articles of utility. " **Crinothene** " is obtainable from stockists of handicraft materials, both locally and from the mail-order specialists in craftwork supplies.

[1] "**Crinothene**" is made from polythene.

There is no adhesive for use with " Crinothene."[1]

Acetate (Plastic): Cellulose acetate is another plastic material suitable for covering lampshades. It is thinner than " Crinothene," and usually has a smooth surface. Acetate is obtainable in a very wide range of colours and surface finishes. It is strong but may crack if it is creased. It is not highly inflammable. Acetate may be jointed by stitching or with a special adhesive—stitching should not be done too close to the edges of the material. It is easily decorated, and may be cut to shape with a sharp knife, razor blade or scissors. It can be marked with a chinagraph pencil.

Fabrics: Fabric covered lampshades are in a class of their own and their manufacture should only be attempted after working with other materials in simple foundation frames. Almost any fabric that will permit the passage of light is suitable for covering lampshades; the most suitable are Satin, Silk, Crêpe, Crêpe-de-Chine, Chintz, Buckram, Gingham, Muslin, Lace and Folkweaves, used separately or with other materials, according to the light diffusion properties of the materials and their suitability of purpose. Covering lampshades with fabrics requires a special technique, which is described in full, later in this book.

Papers: The most popular of these is Parchment Paper, (also known as Vellum). Real parchments and vellums are made from the skins of animals, but most stockists apply these descriptions to papers which are prepared to resemble the real materials. The terms 'parchment' and 'vellum' are now generally used to describe oiled papers of mottled appearance. Parchment paper is easily decorated with oil colours and water colours. It is usually thonged to foundation frames, and is not a suitable material for stitching. Parchment paper can be marked with a pencil, and shapes can be cut with any of the cutting tools mentioned above. It is obtainable in a

---

[1] I stress this, because after mentioning it in previous books, I have received numerous letters telling me I was wrong. I have personally checked every one of the substances mentioned in these letters, and not one of them is capable of jointing **"Crinothene"**. Also, I have discussed this with the manufacturers, who inform me that there is no adhesive for **"Crinothene"**, and, because of the chemical nature of the material, it is unlikely that there ever will be. However, should any of my readers discover any substance capable of jointing **"Crinothene"**, I will be very pleased to put them into touch with the manufacturers.

LAMPSHADE MAKING

wide range of surface finishes and colours, and has many other uses in craftwork.

In addition to the materials described above, there are many other materials suitable for covering lampshades, and their use for this purpose is only restricted by the ingenuity of the individual craftworker. Some skins (if they are treated to render them translucent), are suitable for covering lampshades. Old maps, prints, deeds and wills can all be put to good use and make excellent covers, and there are some other plastic materials which may be used.

The wide range of covering materials of various textures and colours combined with the different types and shapes of foundation frames, afford limitless variety of constructional combinations of originality, and the variety of make-up is further enhanced by the very wide selection range of materials which, although considered to be part of the coverings, are sufficiently decorative to eliminate the need for any extra decoration. These are Braids, Gimps and Bindings of various manufacture which are used chiefly to cover seams and joins in the cover.

Braids, etc.: Braid is a woven material usually manufactured in straight lengths in various colours and patterns—most braids are made from cotton. **Gimp** is a form of braid made usually from fine silk cords, in a variety of widths with fancy edges. **Vandyke Braid** is the name for braid which is shaped in manufacture in zig-zags or wide curves. **Russia Braid** is art silk cord usually used for thonging, but may also be used as a decoration material. **Silk Cord** is heavier than Russia Braid and is mostly used as a decoration material. **Fringe** is made from art silk and cotton, or a mixture of both, and is obtainable in many styles as cut fringe or looped fringe. There are many other materials suitable for finishing.

Thonging: This material is used for attaching some covers to frames; holes are punched in the covering material and the thonging is passed through the holes to bind the cover to the frame. Thonged lampshades are very attractive in some settings, but they are not often made to-day or, at least, not so much as stitched lampshades. Thonging is manufactured of various materials—mostly plastics, but anything which is strong enough to bind covers to frames may be used if it is pleasing in appearance. A leather punch is an ideal tool for punching thonging holes in materials. These are made in the form of hollow hammer punches or plier punches with six-way revolving heads fitted with punches of different sizes. Gauges are obtainable for fitting to six-way punches and greatly assist in the accurate punching of thonging holes.

Binding: This is a material used for covering lampshade frames to provide a foundation on which to sew stitched covers. It is manufactured in the form of tape and is usually described as 'Bias' binding. It is produced in various colours, and it is important to select a binding of a suitable colour to tone with the covering material.

PREPARATION

Foundation frames should be prepared for covering before patterns are made, except in the case of thonged lampshades, the frames of which are to be coated with paint or enamel. Thonged frames may also be bound instead of painted, and this will add to their appearance. The foundation frames of lampshades for stitched covers should always be bound, and the thickness of the binding will make some slight differences to the dimensions of covers. If pattern making is done from uncovered frames, even the very slight difference in the dimensions due to bindings may be apparent in the finished lampshade.

Bindings should be carefully selected to ensure that their colour will tone with that of the covering material. Although in some lampshades, very little of the frame shows in the finished product, in others quite a lot of the frame is visible. Before binding the foundation frame, inspect it carefully. Make certain that there is no rust on the frame, and that there are no kinks or bends in the wires or any distortion of the frame.

All the foundation frame should be bound except the gimbal ring and its supports. If the gimbal ring is covered with bias binding, it may not fit over the lampholder socket. Binding the frames is illustrated in Fig. 1. The frame is a pendant type with the gimbal ring fitted at the top of the frame. The amount of bias tape required for a frame is roughly equal to three times the length of all the wires to be covered. The binding should be rolled as shown in the illustration. An elastic band over the roll will be found useful in controlling the binding.

Commence binding at one of the corners of the foundation frame, and roll the tape firmly round itself. Continue winding

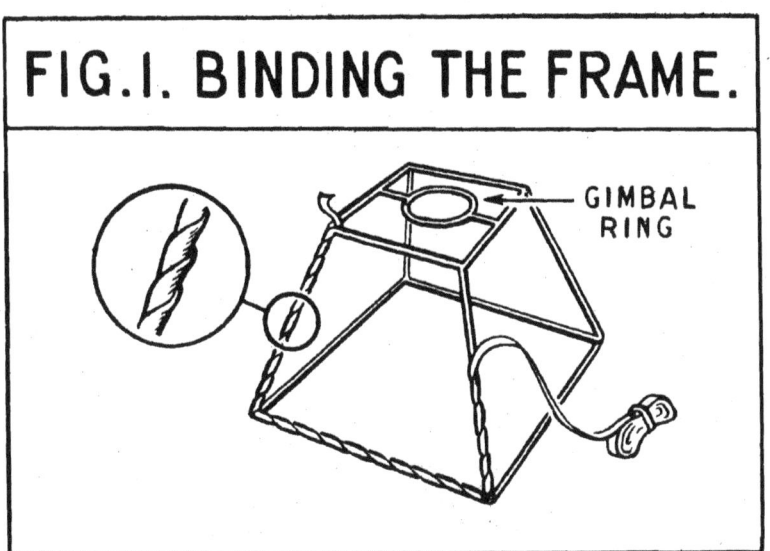

FIG. I. BINDING THE FRAME.

GIMBAL RING

the bias binding round the frame in tightly formed spirals so that each spiral turn covers the edge of the one before. It is not necessary to exaggerate the overlaps, and as long as the wire is completely covered, that is sufficient. Avoid forming lumpy corners and bumpy joins which may show through the covering material. Cover the frame carefully and fasten the ends of the bias binding by sewing or securing them with an adhesive. After binding the frame, a pattern can be made for the cover.

PATTERN MAKING.

This is one of the most important stages of lampshade making. Carelessness in making patterns can only result in badly-made lampshades. Patterns are best made of stout brown paper which has not been previously used and creased. For some lampshades, when they are to be made in quantity, the pattern can be made of stout card. There are two types of lampshade frames; one with supporting side members which divide the frame into panels, and the other which is composed of two separate parts supporting the top and bottom of the lampshade. If the wires of the frame are all straight, it is a simple matter to mark out the pattern from the frame dimensions. If the wires are curved or round as in 'Empire' lampshade frames with separate top and base rings, the making of accurate patterns is more difficult. The Empire shape is very popular; it is conical with a flat top as illustrated in Fig. 2. Also illustrated in Fig. 2 is a simple pattern diagram

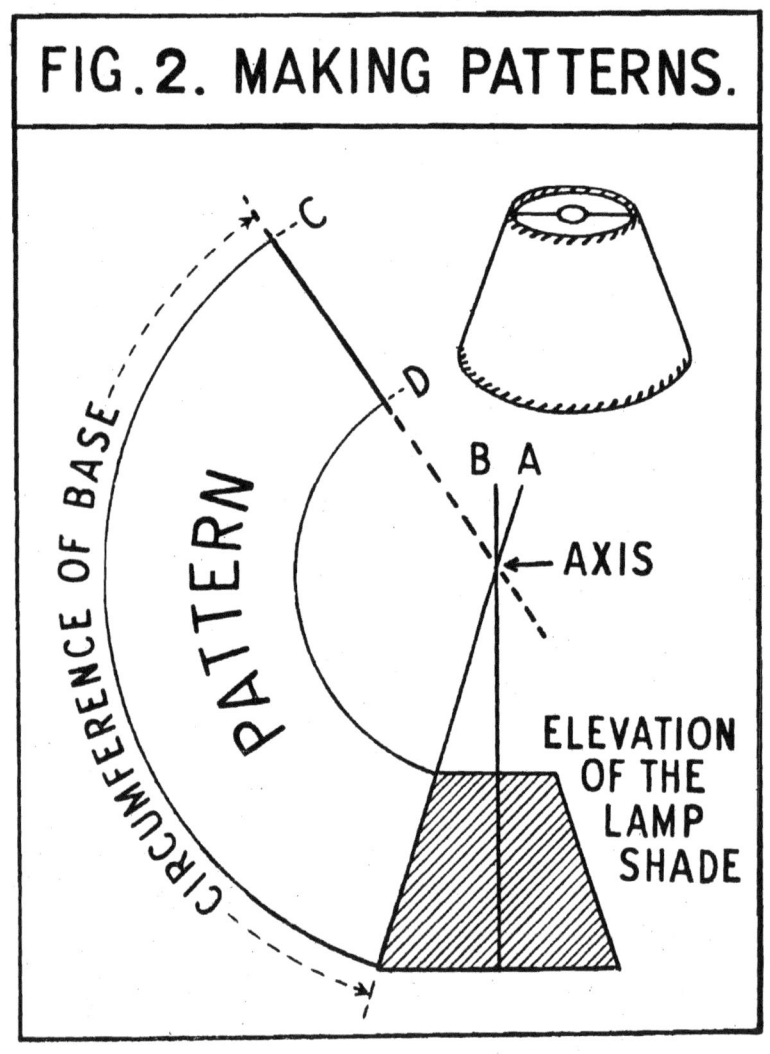

which, if used with the instructions given below, will enable the lampshade maker to construct patterns for the covers of Empire lampshades of all sizes—from the very smallest candle shades to large standard lampshades.

Making Empire Patterns: First draw a true elevation of the lampshade at the foot of a large sheet of brown paper. The elevation should be full scale. The width at the top should be equal to the diameter of the top ring of the frame and the bottom of the elevation drawn on the sheet of the paper should be equal to the diameter of the wire ring fitted to the bottom of the lampshade. It is important to make an accurate drawing. As a guide to the height of the lampshade elevation, add the diameters of the top and bottom rings of the frame, and divide the total by halving it. For instance, if your top ring has a diameter of six inches and the diameter of the base ring is ten inches, giving a total of sixteen inches, the height of the lampshade should be eight inches. This should be considered as a guide only, and lampshades can be made any height to suit the individual requirements of the craftworker.

After drawing the elevation of the lampshade (this is shown in Fig. 2), draw a straight line extending the left hand side of the elevation (line A in the illustration). Draw a second line vertically through the elevation in the middle (line B). From the axis (where lines A and B meet), draw an arc (marked C in the illustration), from the bottom left corner of the elevation to the top of the paper. Draw another arc from the top left corner of the elevation to the top of the paper (this is line D). To complete the pattern outline, take the largest ring of the lampshade frame and roll it along the outside arc. Mark the ring at the starting point and mark again on the paper where the mark on the frame meets line C. From that point draw a line to the axis (where line A meets line B) and the pattern outline should be clearly marked.

This method of making patterns for covers of Empire lampshades is accurate so long as a *true* elevation is drawn to commence with. It should be remembered that the ends of the pattern will meet round the frame, and extra should be allowed where the ends of the material are required to overlap. If the Empire frame has side members it is quite a simple matter to make a cover pattern by rubbing the edges of the frame wires on a rubber stamp pad and rolling the inked frame over a sheet of clean paper. The frame should be marked to determine the ends of the pattern.

Making Patterns for panelled lampshades: After covering the frame with bias binding, place it against a sheet of stout brown paper and press the frame and paper into a cushion or pillow (as illustrated in Fig. 3), and draw round the outline of one of the panels with a pencil. Cut the pattern carefully to shape, and test it against every panel of the frame before using it for marking out the covering material. It may be found that some of the panels are slightly different in size, and allowance for any difference should be made when using the pattern for marking out the material. The foundation frame illustrated in Fig. 3, is the 'Bowed Empire' shape.

FIG. 3. MAKING PANEL PATTERNS

All lampshade patterns should be tested on frames before using them, even if two frames look exactly alike, it should be remembered that they are hand-made and there may be some difference in their dimensions.

If care is taken in making lampshade patterns, there should be no difficulty in cutting perfectly fitting covers. When making patterns, remember to allow for overlapping edges and seams.

After careful selection of the correct size and type of frame, and considering it for suitability of purpose, and selecting the most suitable type of covering material, and preparing the frame by painting it or binding it, and after making a perfectly shaped pattern in stout paper, the more interesting work of construction may be commenced, but it is only by paying careful attention to details in the preliminary stages that one can expect to produce a perfectly made lampshade, and no attempt to cover up bad workmanship in the early part of the work will be successful.

The manufacture of lampshades in great variety is described in detail in the following chapters, commencing with simple lampshades and progressing to those which are more difficult to make.

CHAPTER II

Simple Lampshades — small frames — "butterfly" fitting — inspection — preparation — binding the frame — pattern making — economy in cutting materials — marking parchment — punching thonging holes — thonging the cover sequence — finishing — lampshade with curved sides — preparation, pattern making, marking out and cutting — stitching the cover — how to stitch **"Crinothene"** — attaching gimp and fringes — a thonged and stitched cover — swivel gimbal — pattern making for an Empire frame — joining the vertical edge — finishing — progress in sequence.

THIS chapter deals with the manufacture of simple lampshades. The frame of the first lampshade described, is illustrated in Fig. 4. It has a square top and a square base and is fitted with straight side members at the corners. It is a small frame suitable for a lampshade for a bedside lamp or small wall lamp. It has no gimbal and the method of attachment is a bent wire fitting which is known as a 'Butterfly' fitting. The shaped wires fit over the electric light bulb, thus enabling the lampshade to be swivelled to any angle. The butterfly fitting is a very useful attachment to frames for lampshades which need adjustment to direct light in a desired direction, such as a shade for a reading lamp. The first thing to do is to examine the shade, remove any rust and straighten any bent wires. For the purpose of presenting these instructions in correct sequence the cover is described as being thonged to the foundation frame. Therefore, after checking the frame, it may be painted or bound with bias tape. If it is painted, the colour of the paint should tone with that of the covering material. All the frame should be painted except the gimbal fitting. If desired, the foundation frame may be bound with bias tape, instead of being painted.

If the foundation frame is to be bound, select bias tape of a suitable colour for use with the covering material. Bind the frame carefully as described in the previous chapter. Cover all the frame except the butterfly fitting with tight overlapping spirals of the binding. Form the corners carefully and avoid forming bulky joins. Fasten the ends of the bias binding with an adhesive, or by sewing.

Pattern making comes next. With a simple frame of this type, there is a tendency on the part of the worker to save time by marking the shape of the side-panels directly on to the covering material. But it is a bad habit to get into, and it will be found much better, and more economical in material to make a pattern first. Make the pattern as previously described by placing the bound frame on a piece of stout paper or thin card. Mark round one of the side panels with a pencil. Carefully cut the pattern to shape and test it on every side-panel before using it for marking out the material. If there are any differences in the sizes of the sides, make due allowance for them when marking and cutting out the cover.

Before marking round the pattern on the material, place the pattern in various positions to save waste in cutting. This is general of marking materials for shades of all shapes and sizes. With this simple lampshade, it is obvious that the most economical positioning of the pattern is as illustrated in Fig. 4. There is hardly any waste at all, and although this convenient positioning is not always possible with all types of lampshades, it will be found that a little time spent in trying patterns on materials is well worth while.

The material described for covering this simple lampshade is parchment paper which is easily marked with a pencil. Place the parchment on a firm flat surface, position the pattern on it and mark round the pattern with pencil. Mark all four sides, allowing for any slight difference in their sizes, and cut the material to shape with a sharp pair of scissors, or a razor blade guided by a straight edge. After cutting the material to shape, thonging holes should be punched all round each panel. The holes should be carefully punched with the centre of each hole, from a quarter of an inch to three-eighths of an inch from the edge of the parchment, and the distance between the holes should be about three-eighths of an inch (see Fig. 4).

The position of the holes should be lightly marked on the parchment. If a six-way revolving-head leather punch is used for cutting the holes, these may be cut in all the panels at the same time. Care should be taken to ensure that the same number of holes are punched in each of the sides of the panels. Parchment paper is not usually very thick and there should not be any difficulty in cutting through all four pieces at the same time. The four panels should be placed together and held in place with a strong paper clip, as illustrated in Fig. 4, and then the holes punched. If the punch has become worn and the holes are not cleanly cut, place a thin piece of cardboard over the anvil of the punch, and the holes will be cut cleanly. The holes should be large enough to permit easy passage of the thonging without splitting the material.

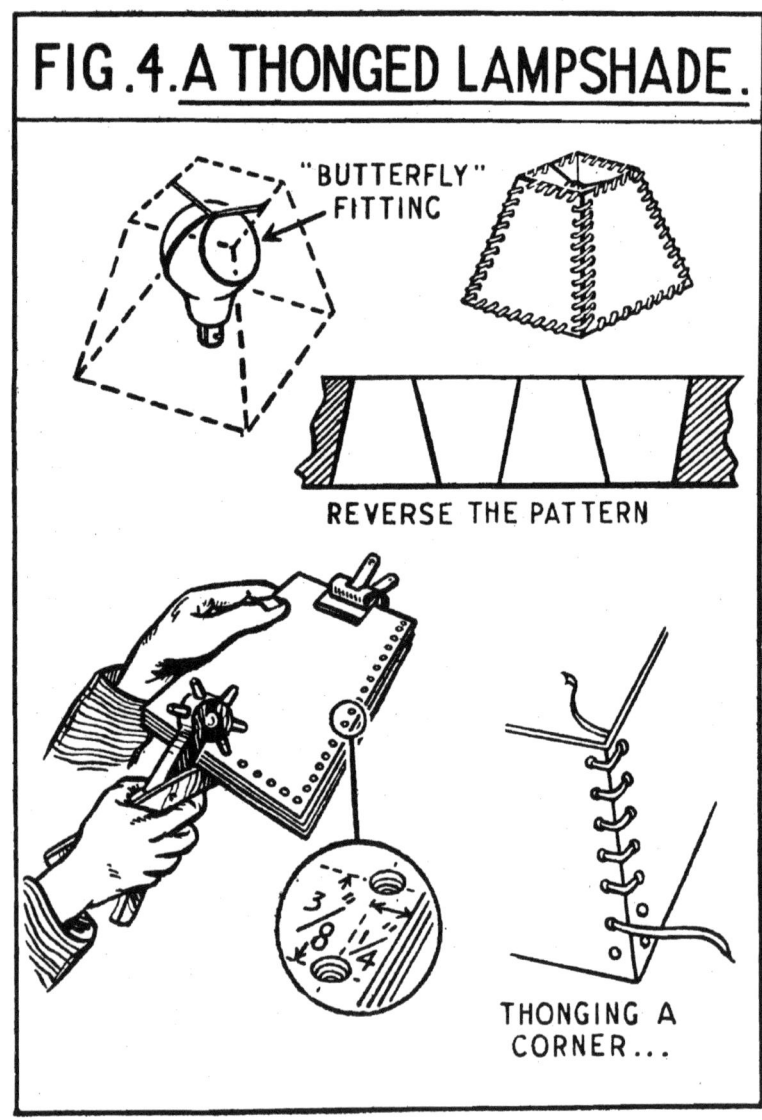

FIG. 4. A THONGED LAMPSHADE.

After cutting the holes in all the panels they can be thonged to the foundation frame. It should be noted that there is a right and a wrong side to " **Crinothene.**" The smoother side of the material should be on the outside of the lampshade. The amount of thonging used for any lampshade is approximately three times the total length of all the wires of the frame. The size of the thonging should be in keeping with the size of the lampshade. As this is a small shade, a very narrow thonging should be used.

Commence thonging by tying one end of the thonging material to one of the wires of the frame, at one of the corners at the top of the frame. Take two of the parchment panels and, commencing at the top of the frame, secure the sides of both panels to one of the upright side members at one of the corners. Pass the thonging from the back of the parchment through the second hole down from the top, bring it to the front and pass it through the coinciding hole of the joining panel, over the back of the corner side-member and through the next hole down in the first panel. Continue thonging down the corner, to the second hole in each panel from the bottom. Cut the thonging about a half to three-quarters of an inch from the parchment and work the end under the thonging inside the lampshade. Undo the knot at the top of the frame, cut the thonging, and tuck the end away neatly.

Thong the edges of all the panels in the same way, then thong the top of the panels to the top of the frame in the same way, with one piece of thonging material. Finish by thonging the bottom edges of the lampshade, cut the ends of the thonging and neatly tuck them away inside the frame.

Care should be taken when thonging, not to pull the thonging material too tight. If undue strain is placed on the edge of the parchment, it may split and break. The thonging need be pulled just tightly enough to hold the material to the frame. This is a very important point to remember when using plastic thonging. Some types of plastic thonging stretch when warm and shrink when cold. The warmth of the hands may be sufficient to stretch the plastic thonging when it is being used, and if it is pulled too tightly, it may shrink in cooling and split the edges of the covering material. If any of the corners of the parchment protrude, they should be trimmed with a sharp pair of scissors. The addition of decorative fringe or braid is not necessary to thonged lampshades in small sizes.

The next simple lampshade described is illustrated in Fig. 5. The frame is very similar to that of the first lampshade except that the corner side-members are curved inwards. It is slightly larger and the gimbal is fitted to the top of the frame. For the purpose of these instructions, the frame is to be covered with **" Crinothene,"** which is to be stitched to the foundation frame with gimp finally attached to cover the joining edges and decorate the shade.

First, examine the frame for rust and kinks in the wire. Bind the frame with bias binding, taking care not to form any bulky joins or corners. Secure the ends of the bias binding, and make a pattern for the side panels. The method of making the pattern is illustrated in Fig. 3. To make the pattern, take a sheet of stout brown paper or thin card, place it against one side of the frame, then place pattern material and frame

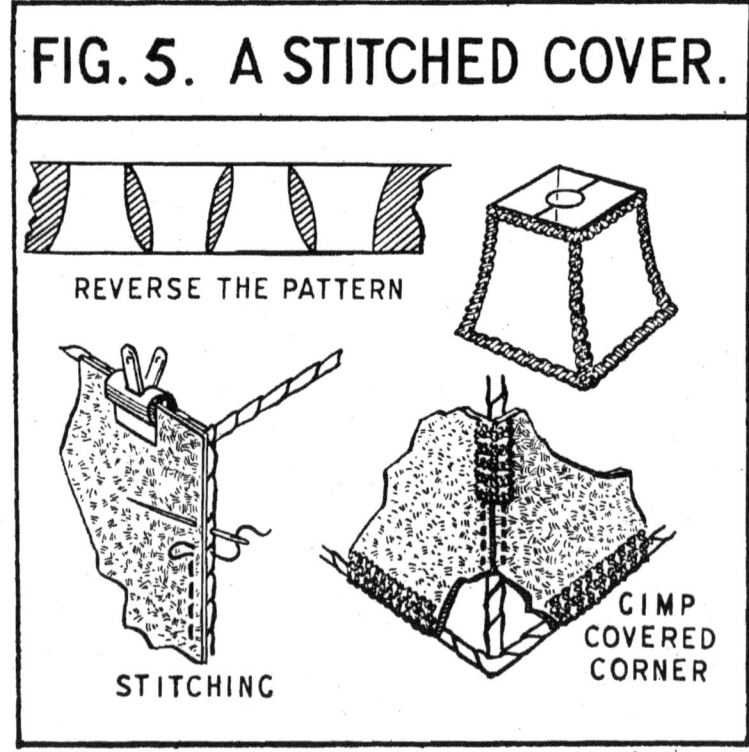

FIG. 5. A STITCHED COVER.

REVERSE THE PATTERN

STITCHING

GIMP COVERED CORNER

against a cushion, so that the pattern paper is pressed firmly against the foundation frame. Do not press the frame too hard on the paper to distort it. Mark round the outside of the side panel. Remove the pattern material and neatly cut the pattern to shape. Try the pattern against all the side panels before using it for marking out the material, and note any slight difference in the size of the panels.

To mark and cut the covering material of **"Crinothene"**, lay the material on a firm flat surface. Place the pattern on the **"Crinothene"** and try it in various positions for economical cutting, and for this pattern shape, the most economical placing of the pattern is as illustrated in Fig. 5. After positioning the pattern, mark round it. **"Crinothene"** can be marked with crayon, chalk, a chinagraph pencil or any of the ball-type pens. Mark accurately round the pattern and cut the material to shape. As the cover is to be stitched to the frame, it will not be necessary to punch holes in the **"Crinothene"** panels, and only one panel should be attached at a time.

Place one of the side panels on the bound frame and, with needle and strong cotton, stitch the panel to the bias binding. For this type and shape of lampshade, it will be found best to commence by stitching along the top of the panel. When sewing, care must be taken not to allow the covering material to 'wander' and to prevent this, paper-clips may be used as illustrated in Fig. 5, to keep the panel in place. Stitch along the top of the panel, securely fastening the edge of the material to the frame, then stitch down the sides, finishing with the bottom edge. Care should be taken not to buckle the panel when sewing it in place. If pattern making has not been accurate, the panel may be a little too small or too large—**"Crinothene"** is not elastic and will not stretch to fill gaps caused by inaccurate pattern cutting. It is important, of course, to use cotton of a colour to agree with the colour scheme of the lampshade. Although the cotton may not be visible from the outside of the lampshade, it may be seen on the inside.

"Crinothene" is easily pierced with a medium-fine sewing needle. The stitch line should not be less than one-eighth of an inch from the edge of the material, but it may be more, and there should not be more than eight stitches to the inch. If more than eight stitches to the inch are used, it may weaken the material at the edges. Stitch holes may be punched round the edges of panels, with a sharp-pointed bradawl, before stitching the panel in place.

After stitching the first side-panel to the lampshade frame, fit the other panels in place and stitch them also to the frame. If strong cotton is used, care must be taken not to pull it too tight if the stitch line is near the edge of the material, or it may break away.

The gimp is attached next. It should be of a suitable colour to tone with the colours of the other material, and it should be wide enough to fold over the corners of the panels and completely cover the joins and stitches in the **"Crinothene"**. Take the gimp, and lay it over one corner of the lampshade, commence stitching at the top of the shade and work down. Use cotton of a suitable colour, and sew the gimp firmly and neatly in place as illustrated in Fig. 5. Cover all the corners first, then stitch gimp round the top of the frame. Use one length of gimp for this and finish off neatly. Stitch another length of gimp round the bottom edge of the frame to complete. When stitching the gimp, sew through the **"Crinothene"** and the bias binding and sew along each edge of the gimp rather than stitching over the inside of the frame wire. If it is required to add a fringe to the bottom of the lampshade, it is not really necessary, but it can be used to suit individual taste. If fringe is added, it should be of a depth suited to the size of the frame, and if gimp and fringe are used, the fringe should be stitched in place before attaching the gimp.

The next type of lampshade described in this chapter of simple shades and covers, is illustrated in Fig. 6. It is the popular Empire type, and for the purpose of these instructions, it is described with a **"Crinothene"** cover which is stitched *and* thonged. The frame is a medium-large one for a table lampshade, and it has a swivel gimbal which is soldered to the top ring of the frame. The gimbal fitting is hinged at each side and the frame may be used for the foundation of a table lamp when the sides are opened to position the gimbal ring at the bottom of the shade, or the fitting may be folded to bring the gimbal ring to the top of the shade in the centre, for attachment to a pendant fitting. The dual purpose of this shade, and its simple shape, recommend it for production in quantity as a commercial venture.

Examine the frame (which is in two parts), make certain

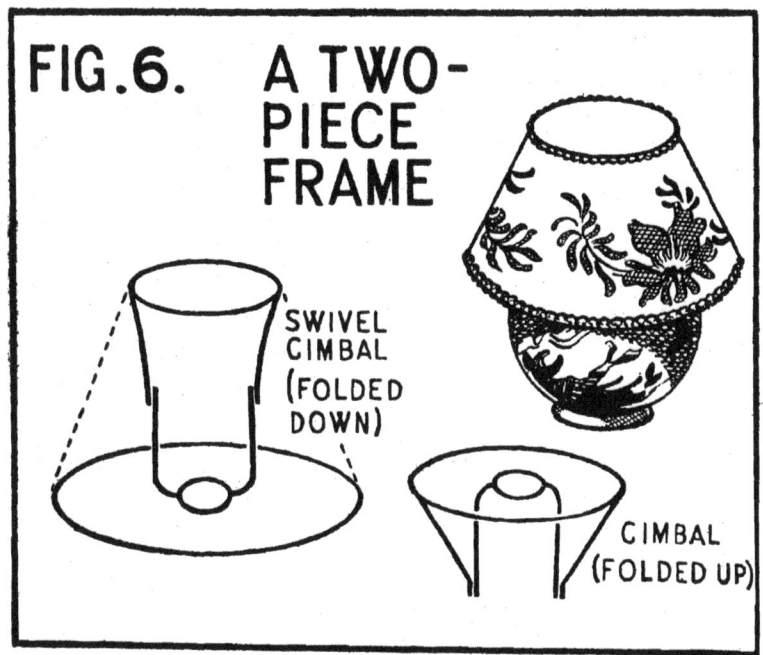

FIG. 6. A TWO-PIECE FRAME

SWIVEL CIMBAL (FOLDED DOWN)

CIMBAL (FOLDED UP)

that the joints are not fractured, that the wire is free from rust, and that there are no unsightly kinks in the wires. Bind the frame with bias binding, carefully and neatly, and cover both parts of the frame except the gimbal ring and hinged side supports. After binding the frame parts, make a pattern of stout paper or card as described in Chapter I, and illustrated in Fig. 2.

Make the pattern carefully and test it round the frame before using it for marking out the material. After making an accurate pattern, place it on the **"Crinothene"**, which should rest on a firm flat surface, mark round the pattern, and allow an extra half-inch at one end of the cover shape for the overlapping vertical join. The cover is to be stitched to the frame at the top and bottom of the lampshade, and the vertical join is to be thonged. Before joining the cover, form it to shape, and with paper-clips or clothes pegs, fasten it to the foundation frame to make certain that it fits perfectly. After checking it for fit, punch thonging holes in the edges of the ends of the cover.

Make certain that the same number of holes are punched in each edge, and position them so that they coincide when the two ends of the cover are joined. The short length of thonging material for joining the vertical edges may be a narrow strip of the **"Crinothene"** cover material cut from the edge of a sheet with a razor blade guided by a straight edge. Thong the vertical join before stitching the cover to the foundation frame. Lace the strip of **"Crinothene"** through the punched holes, pull it fairly tight, but not so tightly as to bend the edges of the cover, trim the ends and stitch them to the cover neatly at the top and bottom.

Place the top ring of the frame in position in the cover and use paper-clips or clothes pegs to hold it firmly. Stitch through the **"Crinothene"** cover about one-eighth of an inch in from the edge of the material, using a medium-fine needle, threaded with cotton of a suitable colour. Do not make more than eight stitches to the inch. Stitch round the top of the cover, fastening it firmly to the bound frame, fasten off neatly. Stitch the bottom of the lampshade next. Insert the large wire ring in the bottom of the cover, and fasten the material securely to the binding round the frame, fastening off neatly.

Stitch gimp round the top of the lampshade to cover the stitches and the edges of the **"Crinothene"**, and use gimp of a suitable width in relation to the size of the lampshade. Stitch the gimp firmly and neatly in position and fasten off with neat ends. If a fringe is required, attach it to the bottom edge of the lampshade, before fitting the gimp.

If care is taken in making the pattern and cutting the material, no difficulty should be encountered in assembling and finishing this popular type of lampshade. Making the three very simple types of lampshades described in this chapter will give the beginner a good grounding in the craft of lampshade making. As in all craftwork, practise is essential, and the beginner should progress in sequence, making certain that he has acquired a sound knowledge of the basic principles, before attempting work of a difficult nature involving the use of costly materials.

CHAPTER III

Flared and fluted lampshade covers: Use of Buckram and Acetate — a flared buckram cover — two-piece frame — preparation — making the cover — simple table for determining dimensions of flared covers — marking out and cutting — assembling — sequence and finishing — variations — other materials. Buckram and fabric — new covers and re-covering — patterns — marking the buckram — joining the materials — cutting to shape — attaching and finishing. A fluted acetate cover — testing for inflammability — foundation frame — gate-legged gimbal — flute patterns — determining dimensions — simple table — guide to flute sizes — alternative method — marking and cutting out — joining the flutes — fitting the cover to the frame — finishing.

THIS chapter deals mainly with the handling of the materials suitable for covering lampshades, Buckram and Acetate, and includes some shapes and styles which progress beyond the very simple lampshades described in Chapter II. The first material described is Buckram.

FLARED BUCKRAM COVER

Buckram has many uses in lampshade making. It may be used alone as a covering material, or it can be used as a stiffening with other materials. It may be decorated by painting, or by stitching to it, shapes of other materials. A very simple buckram lampshade is illustrated in Fig. 7. The wire foundation frame is in two parts consisting of a plain large ring for the base, and two small rings joined together with short side members for the top. The frame is fitted with a swivel gimbal as described in the last chapter. Although the particular frame shown in the illustration is two-piece, foundation frames for this type of lampshade are obtainable, made as one and fitted with side members.

After inspection, the frame should be carefully bound with bias binding of a suitable colour and, as previously described, every part of the wire should be covered except the gimbal ring and supports. When the foundation frame has been bound, the cover should be cut to shape. The buckram cover has two parts; one a large circular piece for the flared body of the cover, and the other a narrow strip for the top of the cover. There is no vertical seam. The dimensions of the narrow strip for the top of the lampshade are found by measuring the depth

FIG. 7. A FLARED COVER.

ATTACHING THE COVER TO THE FRAME

of the top portion to determine the width of the buckram strip which should first be cut in thin cardboard, and the length may easily be found by rolling the strip of cardboard round the top of the frame—cut one piece of buckram to shape. The flared cover is made from one piece of buckram, circular in shape. A pattern need not be made, and the buckram may be marked to shape, by pinning the end of a piece of string through the centre of a sheet of buckram placed on a firm flat surface. The other end of the piece of string should be attached to a pencil, and the length of the string, between pin and pencil, should be equal to half the diameter of the circular cover. The diameter, or the measurement across the circle may be varied according to individual taste, but as a general rule it should be equal to twice the diameter of the larger wire foundation ring, plus the diameter of the ring at top of the frame. I will set this out in table form to make it clear, and base my dimensions on a ring with a diameter of ten inches.

FLARED BUCKRAM COVER

Diameter of base ring	10 ins.
Diameter of top ring (say) ...	5 ins.
Twice the diameter of base ring, plus the diameter of top ring ...	25 ins.

Therefore, the diameter of the circular piece of buckram to make a flared cover of a frame with the dimensions given above, should be 25 inches, and the length of the piece of string between the pin and the pencil should be $12\frac{1}{2}$ inches, as, obviously, the length of the string must be half the diameter. As mentioned before, these dimensions may be changed according to the requirements of the worker, but it is suggested that the beginner should make one or two frames, according to the rule explained above, before changing the dimensions. To outline the cover, hold the string taut, and mark a large circle on the buckram with the pencil. Pencil marks are difficult to remove from buckram so take care not to mark the material unnecessarily. Cut the cover neatly to shape, then mark another circle in the middle of the cover the same size as the top of the frame. Cut this very carefully, and avoid making the hole too large.

After carefully cutting the cover to shape, it can be attached to the foundation frame. The number of curved 'flares' may vary according to the requirements of the individual craftworker, but for a cover of the dimensions given above, eight or nine flares would be suitable. To simplify this description, the number of flares in the cover is eight. It is obvious that care must be taken to form the flares of equal size. If the cover and the large base ring are marked off with equal divisions, equality of the flare sizes will be ensured. Therefore, with a pencil make eight marks equally distanced on the binding of the large ring. Make eight marks on the buckram cover about one-and-a-half to two inches from the outside edge of the material at equal distances apart.

To assemble the lampshade, the bottom of the cover should be stitched to the large base ring first, *not* as in the previous descriptions where the top was secured first. To secure the top of the flared cover before securing the base would place undue strain on the stitches and material which would probably break. To fit the parts together, thread a medium-fine needle with cotton of a suitable colour (buckram may be dyed any colour), place one of the pencil marks on the cover against one of the marks on the large ring, and stitch the buckram firmly to the binding over the ring. Fasten off strongly, then take the opposite mark to the first one, and again place it against the equivalent mark on the base ring and stitch the buckram firmly to the ring. Take the half marks next. These are the marks each side of the cover midway between the two stitch points. Join one side of the buckram shape to the ring, then work on the opposite side of the cover. Stitch the remaining four points in the same way (see Fig. 7). If the buckram is very stiff and difficult to bend, it should be steamed, when it will be found soft enough to manipulate, and on cooling will resume its usual stiffness.

After fastening the bottom of the cover firmly in position to the base ring, move to the top of the lampshade. Place the top part of the frame through the hole at the top of the cover, hold it in place with paperclips or pegs, and stitch both parts firmly together. Finish the cover by stitching the narrow strip of buckram round the top of the frame. All the stitching should be neat and firm. The cover may be decorated in several ways, using the decorative braids and materials previously described. Gimp is suitable for decorating this type of cover, and if it is used, a piece should be stitched round the top of the cover, with another piece round the top over the edges of the flared cover and narrow strip. A third strip of gimp should be stitched round the flared cover all round, about two inches from the bottom edge.

Although it has taken a lot of space to explain the manufacture of this very attractive lampshade, it will be found quite easy to make, if care is taken in the preliminary stages, to ensure that the cover pieces are accurately cut to shape. There are many variations of this type of lampshade, in the number and size of the flares, depth of cover, and decorative treatment, and some other materials may be used in the same way. For instance, **"Crinothene"** could be used to make flared covers;

it will bend quite easily and will keep to shape after stitching. The frame need not necessarily be round—it could be square or any other shape to suit individual taste.

A BUCKRAM AND FABRIC COVERED LAMPSHADE

Buckram may be used with fabrics to make lampshade covers. This combination of materials may be used when the lampshade cover is required to match existing furnishings such as curtains and cushion covers, and almost any kind of fabric may be used with buckram, providing that it is not too light-restrictive. The method described is also suitable for re-covering shabby or damaged lampshades, and the cost of the material is so little that new covers can be made every time a room is fitted with new curtains.

If a completely new cover is being made, it will be necessary to make a pattern. If an old shade is being recovered, the existing cover should be carefully removed and used as a pattern. Care should be taken to ensure that patterns are accurate, and old covers used as patterns should be patched if they are broken. The foundation frames should be carefully examined, and firmly bound with bias tape of a colour suitable for use with the covering material, and this should be done before the patterns are made, and checked against the foundation frame for fit. When it is certain that the patterns fit accurately, they can be used on the buckram. In this method, it is not necessary to cut both materials to shape. Only the buckram—which forms a stiff foundation to the covering fabric—needs to be cut to shape. Place the buckram on a firm flat surface, place the patterns on the buckram and mark round with a pencil. Where more than one pattern is made for a frame with panels of different shapes and sizes, or where several panels of the same size are required, position the patterns carefully, to save waste when cutting. After neatly outlining the pattern shapes on the buckram, turn the material over. As it has to be damped, an indelible pencil should not be used for marking the buckram.

The fabric covering material is affixed to the buckram by making use of the glue used in stiffening buckram, so after turning the material to get the pencil-marked side underneath, soften the glue in the buckram, by wiping over the material with a damp sponge. It is not necessary to use a lot of water—if there is any doubt about the amount to use, experiment on an odd scrap of buckram, before treating the marked piece. After damping, spread the outside cover-fabric over the buckram and with the wrong side down facing the buckram. Use a drawing pin at each corner to hold the material firmly in place, but do not stretch it. Cover the fabric and buckram with a *damp* cloth and press with a *warm* iron. Remove the pressing cloth and go over the fabric again with the iron to smooth out any wrinkles or creases. The buckram-stiffened fabric should be left to dry and harden, before handling it, when it will be found that both materials are firmly welded together.

When the material is dry and hard, turn it over and carefully cut round the pencilled outlines of the pattern shapes. It should be remembered when making the patterns, to allow for any overlaps for joining seams. Overlaps are not necessary at the edges of panel pieces, but for a cover for an Empire lampshade, overlapping should be allowed for, at the ends of the one-piece cover. When the materials are cut to shape, they should be carefully tested against the frame for fitting. In the case of an Empire cover, the overlapping edges may be joined by the use of glue or one of the proprietary adhesives.

Attach the cover to the foundation frame (with the buckram inside the cover) by stitching it to the tape-bound foundation frame. In the case of a panelled lampshade, fit one panel at a time, stitch along the top edge, then down each side edge, finishing along the bottom and taking care not to allow any distortion of the material. In the case of an Empire cover, secure the top of the cover (after joining the vertical seam), to the top of the frame first, finishing with the bottom edge. After fitting the cover securely in place, gimp should be attached at the corners and at the top and bottom of the lampshade, and a fringe may be added if required. It is possible to stick the gimp to lampshade covers of most materials instead of stitching it in place, using one of the suitable proprietary brands of adhesive. Before decorating a completed cover in this way, the beginner should experiment on odd scraps of the material.

There are many other uses for buckram in lampshade making, by itself or with other materials.

A FLUTED ACETATE LAMPSHADE COVER

There are many different names for this material which,

in appearance, is similar to celluloid, but it is *not* celluloid and *is not* highly inflammable. All lampshade materials are inflammable in some degree, but their flash points are *not* such as to make them unsuitable for use as coverings. Should there be any doubt at all in the mind of the worker, it is a very simple matter to cut a small piece of the material and hold it in a flame. If this is done with acetate and the same test is made with a piece of paper or parchment paper, it will be found that the acetate does not burn so quickly or fiercely as the paper. Acetate is obtainable in a very wide range of surface finishes and colours, a transparent variety may also be obtained (often erroneously described as 'mica'), and will be found to have many uses in lampshade making, some of which

FIG. 8. A FLUTED LAMPSHADE

are described in this book. The light passage properties of acetate are quite good, depending on the treatment in manufacture of the material. It may be used for covering lampshades of all types, shapes and sizes, and is very popular for making fluted lampshade covers.

A foundation frame suitable for covering with acetate flutes is illustrated in Fig. 8. It is a medium-large frame, suitable for a lampshade for a large table-lamp or a small standard lamp. Fluted lampshades may be made any size from small candle lampshades, to very large shades. The frame illustrated is fitted with four side members, but two-piece frames may be used for making smaller lampshades. The number of flutes used to make the cover may vary according to the requirements of the craftworker. The lampshade illustrated has sixteen narrow flutes.

The usual preparation should be made by inspecting the frame carefully for flaws and weaknesses, and all the wire of the frame should be bound with bias binding of a suitable colour. It will be seen in the illustration (Fig. 8), that this foundation frame is not fitted with a gimbal, but it has a large recessed ring at the top of the frame which fits over an adjustable 'gate-legged' gimbal (sometimes described as a 'duplex' shade support). The three legs of the gate-legged gimbal are hinged at top and bottom so that they may be adjusted to fit most sizes of frames with standard ring fittings. The gimbal should not be covered with bias binding; it is a separate fitting entirely.

A pattern should be made for the acetate flutes. The number and the size of the flutes may vary considerably, therefore, although these instructions will describe one particular size, they may be considered a simple method of finding other flute sizes.

First, the length of the flute should be decided and this should be approximately (it may vary according to individual requirements) two thirds the combined diameters of both rings of the frame. Therefore, if the lampshade frame measures fourteen inches across the base ring and seven inches across the small ring at the top of the frame, the combined diameters is twenty-one inches, and the flute should be fourteen inches in length. To determine the width of the base of the flute, take the circumference of the large base ring, which of a ring with a diameter of fourteen inches would be approximately forty-four inches. Double that figure of measurement, which would be eighty-eight inches, and divide the total by the number of flutes (16) used for the cover, which is five-and-a-half inches, and this may be taken as the width of the base of the flute. The width of the top of the flute should be approximately two-thirds that of the width across the base—in this case three-and-two-third inches. This general rule is set out below in simple table form, and it should be used as a guide, subject to any alterations to suit the individual worker's needs.

FLUTE PATTERN DIMENSIONS

(based on a round lampshade frame with a top ring of seven inches in diameter and a base ring of fourteen inches in diameter—a cover of 16 flutes).

Length of Flute is equal to two thirds of combined diameters. $7'' + 14'' = 21'' \div \frac{2}{3} = 14''$

Width of base is equal to twice circumference of base ring, divided by number of flutes in cover. $44'' \times 2 = \frac{88}{16}'' = 5\frac{1}{2}''$

Width of top is equal to two-thirds of width of base. $5\frac{1}{2}'' \div \frac{2}{3} = 3\frac{2}{3}''$

An alternative, but perhaps less accurate method, of arriving at flute dimensions is to equally divide the top and base rings by the number of flutes in the cover, and mark the spacing on top and base rings, cutting a piece of card to the required length, curving it and trimming it to a narrowed top, holding the curved card against the marked frame until the required curve of flute is obtained.

After deciding the flute dimensions by either method, mark and cut a piece of stiff cardboard to shape, for use as a pattern. Make the corners of the pattern round (see Fig. 8). Most acetate surfaces can be marked with pencil or one of the ball-type pens. Use the pattern for marking out and cutting, in the most economical way, by reversing the pattern for each alternative flute (Fig. 8). Mark out and cut the required number of flutes. Use scissors or a sharp knife to cut the acetate.

With a thonging punch, cut four holes in each flute about

a quarter of an inch in from the edge, and about one inch to one-and-a-half inches from the ends of the flute (see the illustration—Fig. 8). Make certain that these holes are cut in the same positions in each flute. It is advisable to cut the holes in the cardboard pattern first, and use this over the flutes as a guide to cutting all the flutes in the same place. After cutting the holes, which should be the same size as the bound wire of the frame, make diagonal cuts through the material from the centre of each punched hole to the edges of the flutes.

After punching and cutting, the flutes are ready for assembly. Take two of them, place the face sides of the material together, and stitch through both flutes. The stitch line should be about a quarter of an inch from the inside edges of the punched holes and should extend about half to three-quarters of an inch beyond the holes. The position and length of the stitch line is clearly illustrated in Fig. 8. Join all the flutes together in the same way, by placing facing sides together, and stitching along the edges. Fasten off the stitching securely.

After assembling the cover, it may be attached to the frame. Commence at the top of the cover. Press the wire of the frame through the diagonal cuts, to rest in the punched holes. Do this carefully, to avoid breaking the material, and space the flutes evenly round the top ring of the frame. Attach the bottom of the cover to the bottom ring of the frame in the same way, then with needle and cotton—after spacing the flutes evenly—fasten the acetate to the binding of the frame with a few firm stitches at each junction of frame and cover.

Providing care is taken in the preliminary stages, these fluted lampshades are very easy to make. Acetate is not the only material suitable for making fluted covers, and stiff or medium-stiff material may be used, and this type of lampshade cover may be made, using different materials for alternate flutes. **"Crinothene"** may be used in different colours. Buckram is suitable—or fabric covered buckram—and parchment may be used if care is taken in stitching the flutes together. The cover may be decorated as necessary, by the addition of gimp or braid, or silk cord at top and bottom edges.

CHAPTER IV

" Crinothene " Covered Lampshades: Possibilities of the material — heat-sealing — strength of the joint — vertical joins — tools to use — testing, practise and method — overlapping — surface modelling. **A double cover:** Use of two colours — foundation frame — gimbal adaptor — interlocking shaped pieces — preparation — pattern making — duplicate testing pattern — assembling and tacking the cover — attaching the cover to the frame — alternative edge shapes. **Fitting Curved Panels:** Suitable frame — checking and preparation — pattern making — marking out and cutting — method of ensuring accurate fitting — frame distortion — common faults — decorating and finishing.

THIS chapter describes the manufacture of **"Crinothene"** covered lampshades, and includes a description of the heat-sealing method of jointing **"Crinothene"** (there is no adhesive capable of joining **"Crinothene"**, also a method of making **"Crinothene"** covers by interweaving pieces of the material, thus eliminating *all* vertical joins. The information offered in this chapter, is to supplement that previously given, to acquaint the craftworker with extra knowledge of the possibilities of materials, and to demonstrate how fresh consideration of materials can lead to ingenious uses of them in original presentation.

Heat-sealing "Crinothene": In the absence of any suitable adhesive compound for joining **"Crinothene"**, joining edges of the material may be 'welded' by heat-sealing, and this method of joining is particularly suitable for the vertical seams of lampshades such as the Empire shape and cylindrical shapes. Heat-sealing is done by the application of heat to the material, thus causing it to soften. In hardening, the material fuses, and two joining pieces of the material become firmly welded together. Although the strength of the heat-sealed joint is not quite so great as that of the **"Crinothene"** itself, it is strong enough to withstand the normal stresses and strains to which a lampshade cover is usually subjected. If the heat-sealing is done carefully, the join is practically invisible, and this is a great advantage when making lampshades with only one vertical join, such as the Empire.

It is suggested that the beginner should experiment first with odd scraps of material, to determine application of sufficient heat to effect the fusion of two edges of the material, and to practise finishing the heat-sealing neatly, to simulate the characteristic surface appearance of **"Crinothene"**.

Heat-sealing may be done with a heated tool. An ordinary soldering iron (the type heated over a gas ring), may be used, but to obtain the best results, an electrically heated soldering iron should be used, as it retains heat for quite some time at a fairly even temperature. It is obviously important to use a clean iron. The soldering iron should be just hot enough to *soften* the material (it is not necessary to melt it), and the best heat for this purpose can be determined by testing individual irons on the material.

Take two pieces of **"Crinothene"** and fasten them to a piece of wood with drawing pins or tacks, so that the two edges of the material overlap by about three-eighths of an inch. This is usually sufficient to effect a strong joint, but the amount of overlap may be changed if it is considered necessary. It is possible to join two edges of the material without overlapping them, but the resulting joint is not very strong. After preparing the material, heat the iron, making sure it is absolutely clean and, while it is heating, place an odd scrap of **"Crinothene"** near the end of the bit. As soon as there is any movement of the **"Crinothene"**, turn off the heat and commence working the joining edges of the material. Always commence from the top of the joint and work down, stroking the material rather than pushing the heated iron into it. Draw the iron down the overlapping edge of one piece of the material, and draw it slowly downwards. If the iron is heated sufficiently, the edge of the **"Crinothene"** will soften and spread. If the iron is too hot, it will probably melt a hole in the material. Keep the iron moving and work down the joint. An electrically heated iron should retain heat at an even temperature for enough time to work quite a long joint. In any case, it can always be re-heated if it cools too quickly. It is not essential that the joint should be sealed in one operation. After fusing one edge of the material, turn the pieces over, secure them to the piece of wood, and seal the remaining edge. I suggest the use of wood to work on, because it will not lower the heat of the iron—as would metal. Seal the second edge of the material. Use a small heated iron to finish (a pencil bit, or small metal screwdriver), and model the surface of the **"Crinothene"**, at the join, to resemble the roughened surface of the material.

Allow the joint to cool and harden. After several practise attempts, the craftworker will find it quite a simple matter to heat-seal **"Crinothene"**.

The use of two colours of **"Crinothene"** is possible in making covers for many types of lampshades. In the one described below, two colours are used, and the cover is made up of a double thickness of the material.

A LAMPSHADE WITH A DOUBLE COVER.

This cover style is illustrated in Fig. 9. It is formed over an Empire shape foundation frame, which has a gimbal ring fitted to the top of the frame. Also shown in the illustration is a gimbal adaptor which has a detachable top, held in place by a bolt. It is used for converting a pendant lampshade into a shade for a table lamp.

The double cover of the lampshade is made with four pieces of **"Crinothene"**, ingeniously shaped so that when fitted together, they interlock to form a complete cover. By using **"Crinothene"** of two colours, i.e., two shaped pieces of each colour, a complete cover is formed which when the shade is placed over a lighted lamp, appears to be made of many pieces of different colours. A very simple pattern shape is illustrated, and there are many variations of the idea.

To commence the lampshade, the frame should be carefully inspected, and should then be bound with bias binding of a suitable colour. As two colours are used in the cover, the colour of the binding should tone with both colours of the covering material. For the purpose of these instructions, the cover colours are given as blue and pink. The cover is stitched to the frame and edged with gimp. After checking and preparing the frame, a pattern should be made. Pattern-making for these double-cover lampshades must be *very carefully* done, as inaccuracies, however slight, will show in the finished lampshade, and it is suggested when making these covers for the first time, that a dummy cover is made in thin card, to ensure completely accurate fitting.

Only one pattern is needed for the four pieces of the cover. To make the pattern shape, first mark out two full-size Empire lampshade patterns—it is not necessary to allow for overlaps at the ends of the patterns. Mark out and cut the Empire patterns to shape, fold one very carefully in half, then cut through it. Only half of the Empire pattern is required, but it must be exactly half of the full pattern. Take the half pattern and mark a line down it exactly through the middle (Line A in the illustration—Fig. 9). Mark a line (line B), from the top left corner, to line A at the bottom of the pattern. Mark another line (line C), from the bottom left corner of the pattern to line A at the *top* of the pattern (see Fig. 9). Then, on the other side of the pattern, mark lines D and E, as shown in the illustration. With a razor blade or sharp pair of scissors, cut neatly and cleanly along the lines to remove the portions shown shaded in the illustration. This shaped pattern piece cannot be tested on the frame, therefore it is very essential to mark it out and cut it to shape accurately. As the pattern is to be used four times, it is advisable to make it in card rather than paper.

Cut four pieces of **"Crinothene"** to the shape of the pattern—two pieces of blue, and two of pink. Before the cover is stitched to the frame, it should be assembled and secured

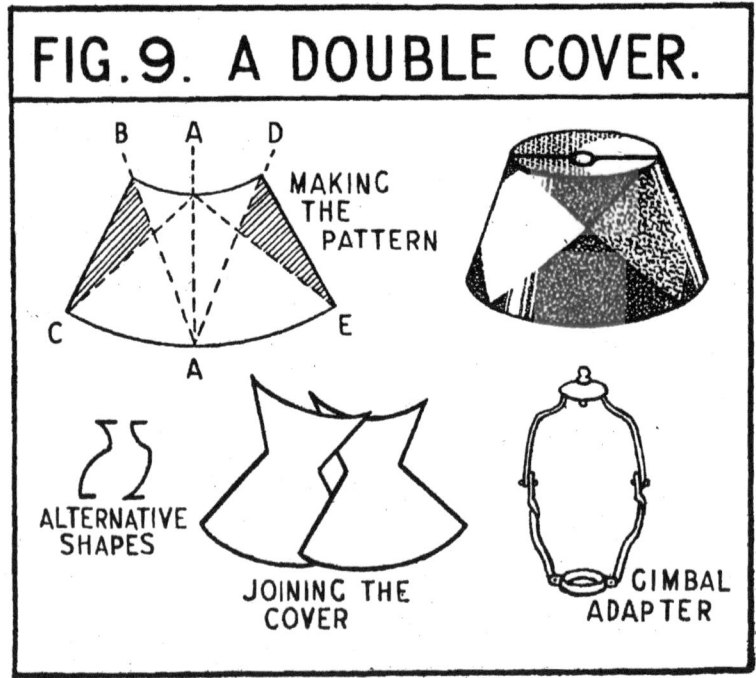

with tacking stitches for checking on the full size duplicate pattern (two patterns were made to commence with). To assemble the cover, take one piece of one colour—say blue—place it on a flat surface. Take one of the pink **"Crinothene"** shapes, place the bottom left corner over the bottom right corner of the blue shape. Place the top left corner of the pink shape *under* the blue shape (see Fig. 9). Take the other blue shape and add it to the two already positioned, overlapping the top and bottom corners alternately, then add the remaining pink **"Crinothene"** shape to the cover, overlapping and underlapping the corners of the material.

To test the cover for fit, place the four interlocking pieces over the duplicate full-size Empire pattern and sew tacking stitches at each of the corners, thus holding the four parts together and maintaining the arc of the duplicate pattern. After tacking the cover firmly, it may be attached to the frame. Overlap the two ends of the cover and tack the corners. Insert the top ring in the top of the cover and hold it in place with clothes pegs or paperclips. Stitch the cover to the binding over the frame in the usual way. Take care not to distort the cover when sewing it to the frame, and do not allow the four parts to loosen. When the top of the cover is attached to the frame, deal with the bottom of the cover and stitch it firmly to the bottom ring. If it is found difficult to stitch through the double **"Crinothene",** stitch holes can be pierced through the material with a sharp-pointed bradawl and this is best done after assembling the parts of the cover, while it is flat, and before joining the end of the cover with tacking stitches. It is suggested to the beginner that to become thoroughly acquainted with assembling and fitting this double-cover, and to avoid cutting materials to waste, a dummy cover should be made in thin card. After securing the cover, the lampshade should be finished in the usual way, by stitching gimp of a suitable width and colour, to the top and bottom edges of the shade. This type of cover may be thonged to suit the requirements of the worker, and there is a very soft translucent plastic thonging available, which is ideal for this purpose. If the cover is to be thonged, the thonging holes should be punched through top and bottom edges of the double **"Crinothene",** after the cover has been tacked and before the ends of the cover pieces are joined. Care must be taken not to allow any gaps to appear between the shaped parts of the cover.

Although the explanation of making these attractive lampshade covers may sound a little complicated, they are really very easy to make after practise and thoroughly understanding how the four cover parts are assembled. It will be found when the cover is assembled and stitched to the frame, that the absence of joined vertical seams does not detract from the strength of the cover, the interlocking edges being so arranged as to provide maximum rigidity. The shape of the cover pieces described is not the only one suitable for making these interlocking covers, and alternative edge shapes for the pieces are illustrated in Fig. 9. The novel appearance and variety of colour shapes and colours, make this type of lampshade cover a useful addition to the range of the commercial lampshade maker.

FITTING CURVED PANELS.

Sometimes in lampshade making, the beginner to the craft finds it difficult to fit materials to curves. Panel shapes have a tendency to 'wander' even when held in position by pegs or clips, and the next lampshade described has a curved frame, selected to demonstrate how to fit panels accurately and prevent the annoyance of gaps appearing in ends and sides of the panels which, although made exactly to the pattern shapes, seem to wander or shrink when stitched in place. This method of ensuring close fit without distortion of the material is recommended to beginners in the craft after they have practised making and assembling some simple lampshades.

The frame illustrated in Fig. 10, is for a pendant lampshade which may be converted for use as a table lampshade by attaching the gimbal adaptor, previously described. It is a stock frame with eight concave panels forming the cover, and eight smaller panels forming a 'skirt' at the base of the shade. For the purpose of this explanation, the frame is described as being covered with **"Crinothene"**, edged with gimp, and trimmed with a fringe at the bottom edge. Although the shape looks a simple one, it is very often with this type of curved panelled lampshade, that the beginner gets into difficulties.

To commence making the lampshade, check the frame joints, see that the wire is clean, and carefully bind all the wires of the frame except the gimbal ring, with bias binding

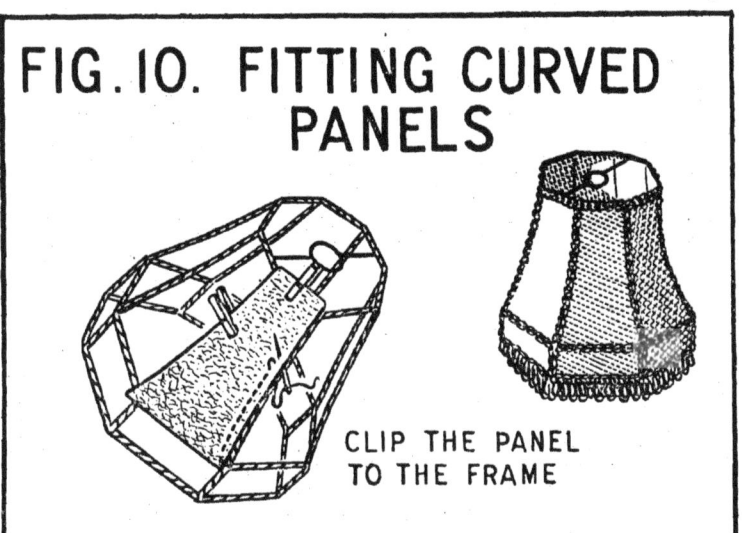

FIG. 10. FITTING CURVED PANELS

CLIP THE PANEL TO THE FRAME

to tone with the colour of the covering material. Fasten off the ends of the binding neatly and firmly. Make patterns next. Make one pattern for the large shaped panels and a separate pattern for the small base panels. Make the curved panel pattern as previously described in stout card by resting the card on something soft, and pressing the frame over the card, so that it is shaped to the curve of the wire. Mark round the panel wires carefully, and cut the pattern to shape. Make the small pattern by measuring the depth and width of the narrow panels and cutting a piece of card to shape. Test the patterns carefully against all the panels of the frame. The side edges of the pattern should cover half the bound wire each side of the panel and at the top and bottom of the panel. After checking the patterns, mark out the material, placing the patterns in position on the **"Crinothene"** in the most economical way. If desired, the strip at the bottom of the frame may be covered with one strip of **"Crinothene."**

After marking the shapes of the large panel patterns on the material, cut one panel only, but instead of trimming close at the top and bottom of the panel, allow extra material of about a quarter to three-eighths of an inch. Take the one panel, and fit it against one of the divisions of the top of the frame, keeping it in place with paper-clips or pegs and allowing the ends of the material to overlap at top and base. Make certain that the side edges of the panel fit exactly over half the tape-bound frame wires. Thread a needle with strong cotton of a colour to tone with that of the covering material, and sew about six to eight stitches on one side of the panel at the deepest part of the curve (illustrated in Fig. 10). Leave the threaded needle in that side of the panel, thread another needle, and commencing at the other side of the panel where the curve is deepest, stitch down to the bottom of the panel. Do not stitch along the bottom of the panel, but fasten off firmly at the corner. Go back to the first needle, and stitch from the commencing point to the *top* of the panel. Fasten off at the top corner. The panel should now be held firmly in place, and will not move while the other half of each side of the panel is stitched firmly to the frame. Leave the tops of the panel untrimmed. Cut the next panel to shape, and attach it to the frame in the same way, commencing each side at the deepest part of the curve, and working up and down the sides. Attach all the eight panels, leaving the tops untrimmed.

This detailed explanation is given to illustrate a common fault of beginners. When covering a lampshade foundation frame with curved panels, it is very easy (especially if the pattern is inaccurate), to cut the panels on the small side, with the result that if they are all cut to the same size, and if there are any differences between the sizes of the panels, the first panel cover is firmly stitched into place but instead of stitching the panel to fit the frame, there is a tendency—however careful the worker may be—to stitch the frame to the panel, and in doing so, slightly bending the wires at the side of the panel. It is obvious that if, after cutting the cover panels to shape, if the wires are bent, even very slightly, the next panel to the one being fixed will be smaller (usually) or larger than the first one, and as the frame is worked round, the very small difference in size in the first place is greatly exaggerated when the last panel is reached. If the last panel of the frame is smaller than the panel cover, it is quite an easy matter to trim the panel to shape, and it should not be 'forced' into the space, or it will buckle. If the last panel space is too large, it is useless to attempt to stretch the material to fit—this can only result in gaps at the side of the panel and undue strain on the stitches. It may be possible to cover any gaps with gimp, to make them invisible from the outside of the lampshade, but they will almost certainly be seen in the inside of the shade, especially if it is to be used over a pendant fitting.

By stitching the edges first, as described above, distortion of the frame can be avoided. After stitching all the sides of the panels, trim the top and bottom of the panels to the shape of the wire, and stitch these edges firmly to the bound wire. Attach the lower panels last—using one strip of the covering material or eight smaller strips. There should be no difficulty in fitting these small pieces to the frame. It is very important to remember that **"Crinothene"** is not elastic and wrinkles or bulges in **"Crinothene"** covered lampshades are only due to faulty pattern cutting and distortion of panel shapes. This method and treatment are also applicable to other firm materials that will not stretch.

After completely stitching the cover to the frame, the gimp and fringe may be added. For the shape described, the vertical seams should be covered first, using gimp of a suitable width and colour. Stitch the gimp neatly and firmly in position, add the fringe next, then stitch gimp round the top edge and the top of the short 'skirt' panels. When attaching gimp to some covering materials, it may be stuck to the material by using a suitable adhesive, such as that used for repairing china. It is possible to attach gimp to **"Crinothene"** with an adhesive, but it is not usually very satisfactory. Although the gimp may appear to be firmly attached to the **"Crinothene"** cover, it may at some later date drop off or break away when cleaning the lampshade. Gimp affords a very quick method of decorating **"Crinothene"** covered lampshades, but it is not *always* entirely successful unless stitched.

CHAPTER V

Fabric-covered Lampshades: Methods and application. A simple lampshade — concave panels — inspection and preparation — binding materials — absence of patterns — ensuring material worked on the bias — use of pins — positioning of pins — stretching the material — covering half the frame — trimming, stitching and finishing — fitted linings. Another method — more difficult frame shape— preparation — fitting separate panels — care in stretching and pinning — sequence of pinning — even tension — stitching, finishing and decorating. A satin-covered standard lampshade — large frame — inspecting and preparing — illustration of points of instruction — different styles of treatment — separate assembly — covering the frame — fitting the lining — pinning, smoothing, trimming and stitching — importance of neatness — shaping the outer cover — marking, cutting and assembling — fitting and fastening the cover — lower panels — decoration and finishing — prowess of the home worker.

THIS chapter deals with the simple manufacture of fabric covered lampshades with sewn covers. Sewn lampshade covers are not difficult to make, if the instructions are followed carefully, and the work is done in correct sequence. Almost any fabric that does not completely block light, is suitable for use as a covering material, providing it is not very openly woven, which would make it difficult to hold stitches. There are many ways of sewing fabrics covers to foundation frames. Panels may be covered separately, or several panels may be covered together, or the cover may be made in one piece for sewing to the frame. The first description is of covering a very simple frame, and the method described may be generally used for covering lampshade foundation frames of all sizes.

The lampshade foundation frame is illustrated in Fig. 11. It is a small frame for a table lamp. It has six panels which curve inwards, and it will be found that frames with concave panels are generally more suitable for covering with fabrics than frames with convex panels. The frame should be carefully checked, bent wires straightened, and rust spots removed, and the joints checked to see that they are not fractured. After checking, the frame should be bound. This may be done with bias binding in the manner previously described, or with strips of the covering material. If strips of the material are used for binding the frame they should be cut about one inch wide,

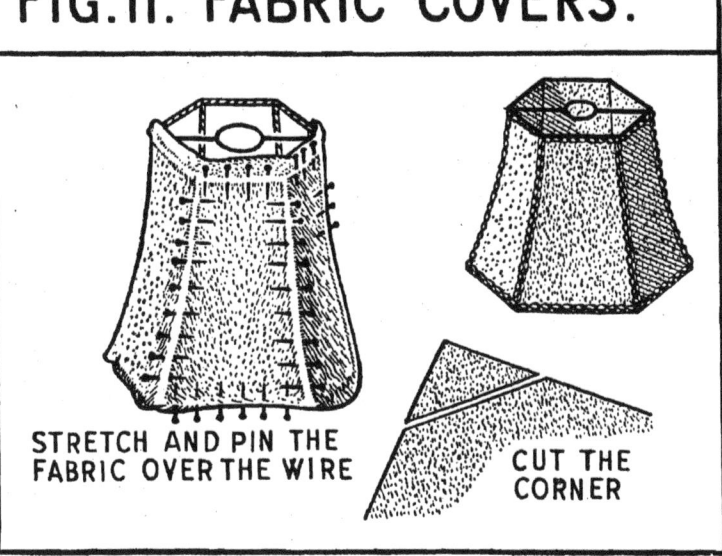

FIG. II. FABRIC COVERS.

STRETCH AND PIN THE FABRIC OVER THE WIRE

CUT THE CORNER

and one edge of the material should be folded over and pressed, leaving the raw edge to be covered by the overlapping folded edge, but if the covering material is very thick, it would be better to use bias binding. Whatever binding is used—self or bias—the frame should be bound carefully, avoiding the formation of lumps and awkward joins, which will show under the fabric cover. To bind the type of frame illustrated, it would be best to bind all the vertical side members separately, firmly and neatly, fastening off the ends of the binding material, and finishing by binding all round the top and bottom edges. After carefully preparing the frame, it is ready for covering. Patterns are not required for the method described here.

There is one very important rule which must be observed when making fabric-covered lampshades. *The material must always be used on the bias*, so that stretch is even in all directions.

The illustration—Fig. 11—shows how the material is shaped over the frame. Commence by folding one corner of the material to form a triangle which can be cut off. This is to ensure that the material is used on the bias, and the trimmed corner should be parallel with the top of the frame when the cover is commenced. Using fine pins, pin the material to the top wire of the frame (as illustrated), then move to the bottom edge of the panel, and pin that also to the bound wire at the bottom of the frame. The pins in the top and bottom edges of the panels should all be vertical. Use plenty of pins to hold the material securely. After fastening the material to the top and bottom of the panel, pin one edge of the panel, fastening the pins through the material and the binding, over the wire of the frame. Pin the left edge of the panel firmly (as shown in the illustration—Fig. 11), then pull the material taut and pin through it at the right edge of the panel. All the pins at the side of the panel must be horizontal. After pinning all four sides of the panel, commence at one of the top corners, pulling the material tautly to the shape of the panel, removing one pin at a time, and replacing it after tightening the material. Work all round the panel, removing the pins, pulling tight, and replacing the pins until the material is tightly shaped over the frame panel, with no wrinkles or sagging corners; the strain should be even in all directions.

After stretching and pinning the first panel, work round to the next. Stretch and pin the top and bottom edges, and the side edge, working all round after pinning, removing pins, stretching the material, and re-pinning until the material is tightly stretched over this panel also. While shaping the material over the frame of this panel, do not allow the stretched material over the first panel to become loose. In this frame, with six small panels, it should be possible to cover one half of the frame completely with one piece of the material. When two panels are covered and pinned, the third panel may be worked, but do not take the next panel round the frame, but move back to the panel before the first panel fitted, stretching and pinning the material firmly over it.

When the three panels have been covered and the material has been evenly stretched to eliminate all wrinkles and creases, trim round the outsides of the three panels to about a quarter of an inch from the frame wire. Thread a needle with strong cotton of a suitable colour to go with the colour of the covering material, and sew the covering material to the tape-bound frame. Sew along the top edge first, turning the edge of the material under, and oversewing the folded edge. Remove the pins as the stitching progresses, but do not take out too many at a time or allow the tension on the material to be relaxed. Sew firmly along the top edge, then down the left edge of the tightened material—removing only one or two pins at a time —then along the bottom edge and up the right edge. While oversewing, trim and neaten the edges as necessary. It is not necessary to sew the material to the two upright side members of the frame in the middle of the stretched piece, and the pins holding the material to these two side-members may be removed, after all the edges have been firmly secured to the frame.

The second half of the frame should be covered in the same way as the first half, by stretching the material on *the bias* over the three remaining panels, pinning round each panel as the work progresses to remove all wrinkles and creases, and finally stitching the outside edges of the piece of material firmly and neatly to the tape-bound frame. It will be obvious from this description that the binding of the frame must be securely and tightly done in the first place. Any loose winds of binding material would not stand up to the strain of the material, and parts of the cover would sag if there were any weaknesses. When the lampshade frame has been completely covered, the inside should be inspected, and any raw edges that may show inside, should be trimmed. If the work is done carefully in the first place, and the edge of the material is trimmed as it is oversewn, there should not be any ragged edges visible in the inside of the frame.

In this method of covering a lampshade frame with fabric, a lining, if required, is easily fitted. Lining effected before the cover is fitted, can be done in exactly the same way by stretching, pinning, tightening, trimming and stitching the lining material over the tape-bound frame, but to save bulky joins at the side members, it is advisable to line only two panels at a time instead of three, arranging the edges of the lining material, so that they are not stitched to the same upright wires of the frame, as the covering material.

If the stitching is done very neatly, the lampshade may not require trimming, but in most cases fabric-covered lampshades of all sizes and types are improved by trimming. For the simple shape described above, narrow gimp or braid should be stitched over the material. First, attach the gimp or braid to upright ridges thrown into prominence by the side members, then sew strips round the top and bottom of the lampshade, covering the edges of the material.

Another method of making sewn lampshade covers is illustrated in Fig. 12. The frame shown is a medium-large one, suitable for a large table lampshade or a small standard shade. The foundation frame is separated into eight panels which have concave and convex curves. The frame is fitted with a 'duplex' ring for attachment to an adjustable gate-leg gimbal fitting. In making the sewn cover, each panel division is treated separately.

The first thing to do is to inspect the frame and bind all the wires with bias binding or strips of the material which is to be used for making the cover. The binding material should be firmly bound round the wire, and firmly fastened off to take the strain of the tight cover. When the frame has been

FIG. 12. COVERING SHAPED PANELS.

PIN HALF-WAY DOWN THE PANEL

made, covering should commence. Remember the most important rule of covering with fabrics is to *always* work the material on the bias so that the stretch is even. Fold one corner of the material over, as previously explained and illustrated, cut the corner off, and place the material over one of the panels with the cut corner level with the top of the frame. Pin through the top edge of the material to secure it to the bound wire at the top of the foundation frame, with the pins placed vertically. Use plenty of pins to ensure holding the material firmly. Up to this point, the instructions have been almost the same as those given for making the first fabric-covered lampshade, but from here they differ, as the shade previously described had concave panels only.

When the top of the material is firmly affixed to the top of the frame, pin at the bottom of the panel, but do *not* pull the material too tightly. Merely insert a pin to fasten the centre of the material to the middle of the base panel wire as a guide. It will be seen from the shape of the foundation frame that if the bottom edge of the material is pinned firmly, and the material is stretched, it will leave a gap between the foundation frame and fabric at the upper part of the panel, which is concave. To fit the covering fabric over the curved panel, work down both sides of the panel wires at the same time. Use plenty of pins and insert them horizontally through the material and the frame binding. Place a pin through one edge of the panel covering, then pull the material tight, and insert a pin in the other edge of the panel opposite the first pin. Pin again under the *second* pin inserted, then stretch the material from the other side of the panel and insert the fourth pin (the pins are numbered in the illustration—Fig. 12—to clarify this explanation). The fifth pin should be inserted under the fourth pin. Continue working in this way, inserting two pins at each side of the panel, and pulling the material tight as the pinning is done, to a point halfway down the panel, where the concave curve becomes convex. When pinning the top half of the panel, move the bottom pin as necessary, merely using it as a guide to the centre of the panel covering. After passing the forward curve, the bottom edge of the panel covering should be firmly pinned to the binding at the bottom of the frame. Insert the first pin at the bottom, in the middle, then work from this pin outwards to the panel edges, inserting a pin alternately each side of the first pin, pulling the material taut all the while. When the bottom is firmly secured, pin the bottom half of the edges of the covering to the wire covered frames at the sides of the panel. Care should be taken at every stage, to ensure that the tension of the material is even in all directions.

Go all round the panel, removing a pin at a time and pulling the material tight, to smooth out all wrinkles and creases. When the panel is smooth and tight, trim the material to a quarter of an inch of the wires, and commence stitching. Start at the top left corner and use strong cotton of the same colour as the covering material. Turn the edge of the material under and oversew the fold to the frame binding. Stitch all round the edge of the panel, neatly and firmly, removing one or two pins at a time, and maintaining an even tension of the covering fabric. After working all round the panel, fasten off firmly and neaten all raw edges inside the lampshade. When experience is gained with practise, it will be found possible to neaten the edges as the panel is sewn in place.

The remaining seven panels are covered in the same way as the first, taking care to work the material on the bias and maintaining even tension of the panels. When the cover is finished, it should be decorated with braid, gimp or silk cord. For a shade of the size and shape of the one described, a wide gimp would be suitable to cover the joins between the panels, and to edge the frame. A fringe could be attached, if required.

The third fabric-covered lampshade described is rather more difficult to make, than the two previously mentioned. The frame is illustrated in Fig. 13. It is a large frame for a standard lampshade, and is fitted with a 'duplex' ring. It is a fairly simple shape to cover, but to illustrate another method of fitting fabric covers, it is described as being covered with white satin. The top edge is trimmed with silver-coloured braid, the two bottom edges are also trimmed with silver braid, and the bottom edge will have a deep fringe of silvery silk cord, but the upright seams of the body of the cover are not to be covered with braid or gimp. Obviously, such a lampshade of this description would only be suitable for use with a complementary furnishing scheme, and the purpose of describing this lampshade, is to illustrate some points of instruction for making all types of fabric-covered shades—for this purpose, the quality of the material, colouring, shape and style of trimming could be changed to suit a particular requirement.

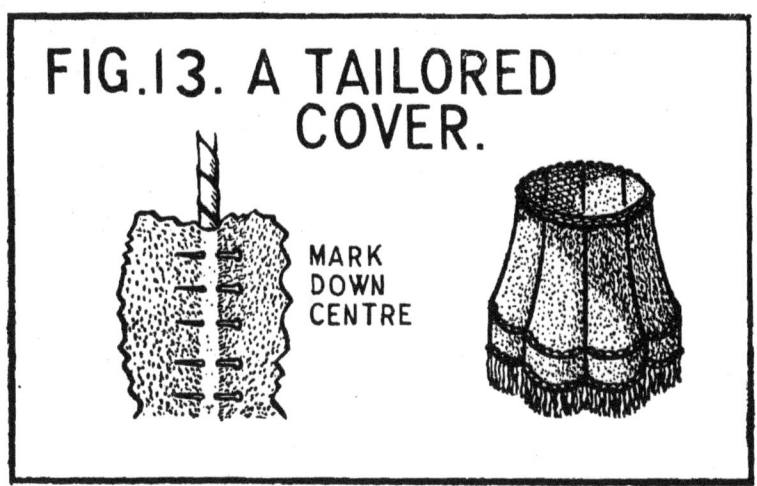

FIG. 13. A TAILORED COVER.

MARK DOWN CENTRE

Two different styles of treatment are described in making the sewn cover. The top part of the covering is marked to shape over the foundation frame, but it is not stitched direct to the frame. It is assembled separately and fastened to the frame as one piece. The panels in the lower half of the lampshade are fitted and attached directly to the frame. The lampshade is lined, and, for use with satin, a fine texture such as Lawn, is suitable.

The foundation frame should be very carefully checked for inaccuracies and faults, and although care in checking is necessary as a preliminary to covering lampshades with any type of material, extra care should be taken when using expensive covering materials. After checking and rectifying any faults, the frame should be carefully bound with bias binding of a suitable colour, or with strips of the lining material. Use of the lining material is preferable to the covering material. Bind the frame carefully and firmly. Cover all the upright wires first, then bind the three wires running round the frame. The foundation of binding must be attached very firmly and ends should be fastened off securely.

When the preparation has been satisfactorily completed, the work of covering the frame should commence. First, the lining is attached. A corner of the lining material should be cut (as previously described), to ensure that the material is attached on the bias. The treatment of the lining is as previously described. The material should be carefully fitted over each panel, from the *inside* of the frame, and secured with pins. The material should be kept very tight, by working round each panel, removing pins and stretching, to pull out any wrinkles or creases, before replacing the pins. The top panels should be lined first, and the panels at the bottom of the frame lined last. Two or more panels may be lined together, according to the size of the lining material. Great care should be taken in trimming, turning and sewing the edges of the lining material to the foundation frame. Although it is unlikely that much of the work will be visible when the lampshade is in use, neatness in attaching the lining is essential, especially if the lampshade is being made for sale. Trim and fold the edges of the lining material, removing one or two pins at a time, and sewing with fine neat stitches. The edges of the material should be arranged to come halfway over the supporting wires. The lower panels of the frame will be found quite easy to line separately, using small pieces of material. After lining has been completed, trim any raw edges of the material inside the lining (that is from the outside of the frame).

When the lining has been satisfactorily fitted, the main cover may be made. Each panel should be fitted separately over the frame. Commence with any of the panels. Cut a triangular corner of the satin to work the material on the bias, pin through the top edge of the material to the top wire of the frame, using *very* fine pins with the right side of the material outside. Pin the bottom edge next, keeping the material smooth. Pin the edges of the panel, then work carefully round it, moving pins and stretching the material, until the panel is tightly and smoothly covered. Arrange the pins as shown in the illustration, so that the material may be marked where it covers the wire. The outline of the panel should be marked on the material and this is best done with chalk which can be brushed off when the cover has been stitched. Mark all round the panel over the middle of the bound wires. Remove all the pins and trim the material to the panel shape at the edges, allowing an extra one quarter to three-eighths of an inch for turning. The top and bottom need not be trimmed at this stage. As the panels are stretched, marked and cut, they should be kept in the order of making so that, when fastened together, each panel covering is stretched over the actual panel to which it was fitted. This is important because there may be some differences in the sizes of the panels. After cutting all the eight panels of the top of the cover, they may be fastened together. Fig. 14 illustrates how the panels are joined on the wrong side of the material. Accuracy in stitching is essential and is best done on a sewing machine. Stitch the eight panels together, press and neaten the seams and fasten off firmly.

After assembling the top of the cover, it should be fitted over the lined frame. This should be done carefully, ensuring that the seams fit exactly over the upright side-members. Place the cover over the frame as far as it will go, then work round, gently pulling each panel down until the cover is smooth and unwrinkled. Use fine pins to keep the bottom edge of the cover in place, then pin round the top edge through the frame binding. Keep working round the lampshade removing one pin at a time and stretching the cover smoothly over the frame. If the panels were sewn together properly, there should be no wrinkles across the material. Care should be taken when fitting the cover not to ruck any of the pressed seams where they cover the frame wires. When you are fully satisfied that the cover is perfectly fitted, commence stitching the top edge of the satin to the frame binding. Trim and fold the material. Stitch neatly and firmly, removing one or two pins at a time and keeping the tension on the material. Stitch all round the top of the cover, then sew the bottom of the cover to the binding, over the uppermost wire of the lower panels. Keep the material smooth and taut while sewing, and fasten off firmly.

When the top part of the cover has been fitted and sewn,

FIG. 14. JOINING THE PANELS.

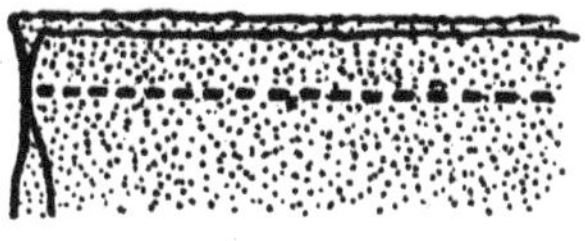

STITCH THROUGH THE WRONG SIDE

the small lower panels should be covered. These small panels may be covered singly with pieces of satin left over from the main cover. Work one small panel at a time, making certain that the material is used on the bias. Pin along the top edge first, then stretch the material and pin the bottom edge, pinning the sides of the panel last. Work round the panel several times, moving the pins and tightening the material. Trim the edges of the panel with a sharp pair of scissors and stitch the edges of the material to the frame, removing one or two pins at a time, and trimming and folding the edge under, as the sewing progresses. Cover all the eight lower panels. After the cover has been completed, the braid should be attached.

Stitch the silver braid to the top of the lampshade first, covering the edges of lining and satin with the braid. Fasten the ends of the braid neatly. Then affix braid to each upright edge dividing the panels. Fasten the ends neatly. Stitch braid round the top edge of the lower panels covering the joins of the material. Attach the fringe next, to the bottom edge of the lampshade, and finish by sewing braid over the top of the fringe.

The manufacture of these 'luxury' lampshades is not beyond the capability of the home worker, providing that the work is done in sequence and each stage of the work is carried out carefully. It is repeated that lampshades of the type described above would be suitable only for use amid certain surroundings, but the knowledge presented in the instructions is generally useful to the lampshade maker for making all classes of sewn fabric covers. There is unlimited scope in making large lampshades of this type to order, and it can be a very profitable pastime.

CHAPTER VI

A Parchment and Velvet Cover: Simple foundation frame — cleaning real Parchment — removing wrinkles and creases — care in handling — preparing the frame — attaching the velvet corner pieces — pinning, trimming and sewing — marking and cutting the parchment panels — attaching the panels — braiding and finishing. **A shade for a Bed Lamp:** Avoidance of a common fault — enclosed tops — preparation — using odd pieces of material — patterns — two-colour cover — attaching the acetate — decorating and finishing. **Empire shade with modelled edge:** Suitable frame — " Barbola " edges — assembling the cover — testing for fit — overlapping ends — joining the vertical seam — fitting the cover — attachment to the frame — the " **Barbola** " edge — depth — working the material — attaching, modelling and finishing.

THIS chapter deals with lampshade making in general, and includes descriptions and instructions for shades and covers of all kinds and types, each one described to illustrate a particular feature of making lampshades.

The first lampshade described has a very simple foundation frame (illustrated in Fig. 15), which is to be covered with parchment and velvet. The parchment described is not imitation parchment paper but real parchment in the form of old maps, deeds, wills, etc., which are very suitable for covering lampshades for use in lounges and dining rooms. Old parchments, when obtained, are sometimes stained and wrinkled, and it may be found necessary to clean and smooth them before use. If parchment is washed in hot water, and dried before a fire, it will shrivel and go hard, thus rendering it unsuitable. The material—which is thin skin—should be cleaned very carefully to preserve any writing on it, which is necessary to the character of these attractive lampshades.

Before cleaning, a simple test should be carried out to ascertain that the writing ink is fast, and will not be damaged. To test for fastness, wet a small part of the ink, cover the part with blotting paper and rub over the blotting paper with the wrong end of a pencil. Remove the blotting paper and if it is clean, the ink will withstand the cleaning process.

The material should be cleaned first, and this may be done by mixing a *weak* solution of oxalic acid in water, and washing the parchment. Fasten the parchment to a smooth surface

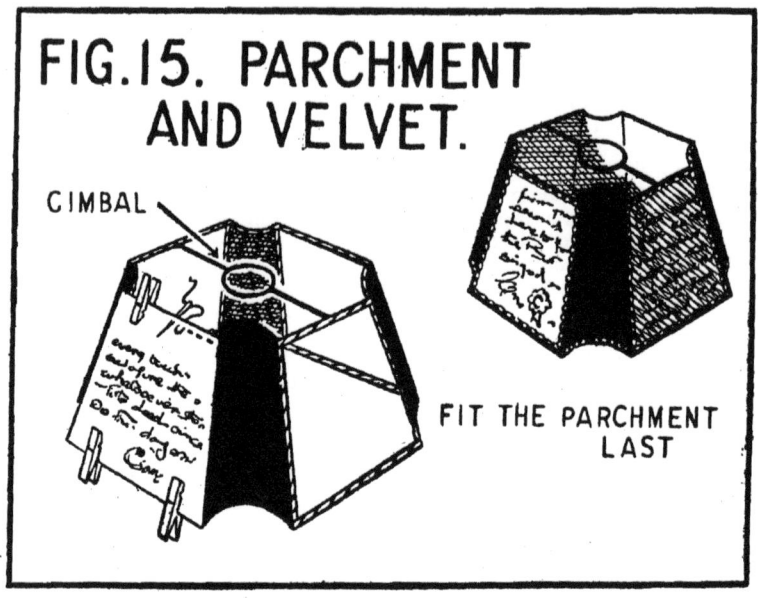

FIG. 15. PARCHMENT AND VELVET.

CIMBAL

FIT THE PARCHMENT LAST

and wash it gently and quickly with a sponge dampened with the solution. Test the cleaning fluid on a corner of the material, before applying it to the whole. Work quickly, and as soon as the material is clean, dry it with blotting paper. Clean both sides of the material, taking care not to make it too damp. After cleaning, wrinkles and creases may be removed. To render the parchment smooth and supple, place the deed or map or whatever the document is, *face down* on a sheet of clean blotting paper resting on a firm flat surface. Beat up the white of a fresh egg to which should be added a few drops of Oil of Cloves, and whip the mixture to a froth. Using the fingers, spread the mixture all over the back of the parchment, and rub it in with the finger tips, paying particular attention to any folds and heavy creases. Smooth the parchment, pin the corners and cover it with oiled silk. Place a board or piece of stout cardboard over the silk, weight the board and allow it to stand for twenty-four hours. After that, remove the board and silk, cover the back of the parchment with a piece of fine textured cloth (not damped) and press with a *warm* iron until all the wrinkles have disappeared. This cleaning and smoothing process must be done very carefully, and although it is a lengthy one, it is very effective in restoring dirty and wrinkled parchment.

After preparing the materials, the frame should be checked and bound. The foundation frame illustrated in Fig. 15, is a very simple one with concave corners. Parchment is used to cover the large side panels, and velvet—maroon, brown, wine or any rich dark colour—to cover the corners. After binding the frame with material of a suitable colour to tone with both the covering materials, a pattern should be made for the side panels, which are to be covered with parchment. Mark the pattern outline on thin card, and cut it to shape, and check it against all the sides. Attach the velvet to the foundation frame before fitting the parchment panels. To do this take a strip of the material and place it over one of the concave corners. Pin through the material and the binding at the top and bottom edges of the frame. Pin the side of the strip of velvet to the upright corner wires, and, as previously described, work round the corner-piece, tightening the material and adjusting the pins. Care should be taken not to strain the material too tightly across the narrow corner piece and the greatest tension should be down the material, to prevent the middle of the strip becoming bowed. After fastening the velvet strip shapely and firmly to the corner wires, trim it, leaving enough of the material to turn over at the edges. With a needle and strong cotton of a suitable colour, stitch the velvet to the frame binding. Trim and neaten the edges as the sewing progresses, and only remove one or two pins as necessary, to maintain the tension and shape of the material. Fasten off firmly and cover the remaining three corners in the same way. When all the corners have been covered with velvet, the parchment should be fitted to the sides. Use the card pattern on the parchment, position it carefully to effect the maximum economy in cutting the material, and mark round the pattern with a pencil. Cut the parchment panels to shape with a pair of sharp scissors or a razor blade guided by a straight edge. The parchment panels should be stitched to the foundation frame. Care must be taken not to break the material at the edges of the panels, and it is advisable to pierce stitching holes first, near the edges of the panels, with a fine-pointed bradawl. Use a medium-fine needle and strong cotton, to attach the parchment panels to the frame. Stitch firmly, but do not pull the cotton too tight, or it may break through the edges of the material. Use paperclips or clothes pegs to hold the panel in place while it is being stitched. Stitch the top edge first, then the bottom edge, finishing with the side edges. It should be remembered that the material will not stretch, and no attempt should be made to pull it to the shape of the frame, if the panel has been cut too small. This should not happen if the pattern has been carefully made and *checked* against the frame before using it to mark out the shapes of the panels. Sew the four parchment sides to the frame. To trim this lampshade with its mellow parchment sides, and rich velvet corner pieces, gold braid, or brown braid with gold threads in it, would be very suitable. The upright joins should be treated first, neatly shaping the braid over the corners to cover the edges of the parchment and velvet. Care should be taken when sewing the braid to the cover, to sew through the material under and over, and not over the inside of the bound wires. After braiding the upright edges, finish by trimming the top and bottom edges of the lampshade, using a single strip of braid for each edge. This mixture of materials in lampshade making, may be applied to other combinations of materials and for covering very many types, shapes, and sizes of lampshade frames.

The next lampshade described is illustrated in Fig. 16. It is a shade for a bed lamp, and has been selected to illustrate the avoidance of a common fault in lampshade making. Very often, when a small lampshade is made, the top of the shade is completely enclosed with the covering material, and in a small shade, the electric light bulb must be in fairly close proximity with the cover. Therefore, if a lamp bulb of too high a voltage is used in a small lampshade of this kind, the heat generated by the lighted bulb is bound to have a deleterious effect on the covering material—whatever form of covering is used. The material will become scorched and burnt. It may melt, or crack or warp, even if, as explained in a previous chapter, a lamp bulb of a power suitable for the size of the lampshade is used. If the top of the lampshade is enclosed, the cover will have a short life; part of the shade at the top must be left open to permit the hot air generated by the heated bulb to escape. In the case of the lampshade illustrated, it is obvious that the front and top should be covered in one piece. The foundation frame has two sides

FIG. 16. A SHADE FOR A BED-LAMP.

LEAVE THIS PART OPEN

which should be completely covered. Therefore, the only means of escape for heat is through the back of the lampshade, and if the illustration is studied, it will be observed that the back of the frame is separated by a horizontally fitted wire near the top, and the covering material at the back of the lampshade should only extend from the bottom wire at the back to the horizontal member, thus leaving the top of the back open for the escape of heat.

To make the lampshade, first inspect the foundation frame, checking for fractured joints and bends in the wire, then bind it firmly with bias binding suitable to tone with the covering. Cover all the frame, except the gimbal. As this is a bed-head lampshade, and suggests relaxation and ease, we will make it look comfortable and restful, using a material coloured a soft pastel shade to cover it, and trimming the cover with gimp and a short fringe. Acetate or **"Crinothene"** may be used to provide a softly diffused light, but for the purpose of this description, acetate is selected as the covering material. It is possible, when covering small frames, to use odd pieces of material left over from making large shades. If the frame shape is studied, it will be observed that there are two small sides and the top and front are divided into three by the use of two curved members which are shaped at the back of the frame in the form of a hook to fit over the head of a bed. Therefore, we can use six pieces of material (including the back), to cover this small frame, and use up odd pieces, provided that suitably coloured remnants are available.

After inspecting and binding, the foundation frame patterns should be made. Only one pattern is required for the ends of the lampshade, another pattern is required for the centre piece of the top and front, and one for the end pieces of the front. It is repeated that even simple shapes like those illustrated in this frame should not be marked directly on to the covering material. The pattern-making habit should be cultivated and used every time, except in the case of sewn fabric covers, where the material is fitted direct to the frame. After making the patterns in stiff card, test them on the frame and note any slight inaccuracies in size. The style of this lamp lends itself well to the use of more than one colour of covering material. The large centre panel in the front of the shade, and the two quarter circles should be covered in material of the same colour, with the two end panels of the front, and the three-quarter back, covered with material of a contrasting colour. Colour selection is a matter for individual consideration, but for the purpose of this description, and to identify the parts, the two colours described are peach and ivory, and these pastel colours are obtainable in acetate. Also obtainable in acetate is a surface finish which gives the material an appearance not unlike that of watered silk. So we will describe our bed-head lamp, as being covered with odd pieces of peach and ivory acetate with watered silk surface finish. As the material has a definite grain, this should be considered when marking out the covering, and the wavy lines of the watered silk surface effect, should be across the widest parts of the cover.

Mark round the patterns on the material, positioning the patterns so that the 'grained' surface markings run in the same direction on all the six pieces of the cover. Cut the acetate to shape with a pair of sharp scissors. Straight cuts can be made in acetate by scratching the material with a pointed tool, guided by a straight edge, and folding the material in the direction of the scratch-line, when it will be found to split neatly. Acetate may be stitched with a medium-fine needle, but it is advisable to pierce stitch holes in the material, before commencing to sew. The stitch holes should not exceed six to the inch. Commence by stitching the three-quarter back, to the foundation frame. Affix it firmly, then attach and sew the centre front panel in position. Attach the two end panels to the front of the frame next, and sew the ends last of all. Fasten off firmly, and stitch gimp over the joins in the front of the cover and over the front edges at the ends. Stitch one length of gimp to the back edge of the shade, then add a short fringe to the bottom of the shade. Remember always, when covering small shades, to leave an aperture for heat to escape.

The next lampshade described is a simple Empire type with a swivel gimbal attached to the top wire of the frame, for use with a table lamp-base. The description is of a plain cover of parchment paper, and the chief feature of the lampshade is its modelled **"Barbola"** edges. I would like to make it quite clear that many of the modelled lampshade edges are not done with **"Barbola"** and there are many brands of modelling pastes. The word **"Barbola"** is a registered trade mark of **Winsor and Newton Ltd.**, the manufacturers of the original **"Barbola"** Paste, and through constant usage, the term 'barbola' work, is loosely applied to all forms of paste modelling. However, to avoid any confusion, **"Barbola" Paste** is described as the material used to make modelled edges on this parchment covered lampshade.

There are several ways of assembling covers to make lampshades with modelled **"Barbola"** edges. These instructions describe one of the most effective methods. In this, the lampshade frame need not be bound with bias binding, but it should be checked for fractured joints, rust spots, and kinks to ensure that it will make a reliable foundation. After checking the frame, a pattern should be made, and this is the ordinary Empire pattern included in previous descriptions, but, when using the pattern in marking out the shape of the cover on good quality parchment paper, allow an extra three-quarters of an inch at the top and bottom of the cover, and allow an extra one-quarter of an inch at one end of the cover, for overlapping the vertical seam. The extra material at the top and bottom edge of the lampshade cover is lapped over the frame. The cover shape should be tested on the frame before joining the vertical seam. To do this, shape the cover inside the frame wires, mark and cut the material to fit through the gimbal supports—this is illustrated in Fig. 17—and position the top and bottom rings at about three-quarters of an inch from the top and bottom of the cover, holding them in place with spring-clip clothes pegs. Mark the overlapping seam lightly with a pencil, and lightly mark round the outsides of the top and bottom seams, also with a pencil. Remove the pegs and dissemble the cover. Cut V-shape notches in the edges of the material at the top and bottom of the cover, from the edge to within a quarter inch of the pencil lines marked round the frame, and trim the end of the cover, if the overlap is more than three-eighths of an inch. The cover can now be assembled and attached to the frame. Join the vertical seam first, as illustrated in Fig. 17. Place the join over a piece of thin wood, apply liquid glue under the overlap, and fasten the two joining edges together. Use a drawing pin at each end of the vertical join, wipe off any surplus glue, place a clean piece of wood over the top of the join and hold the pieces together with a 'G' clamp, gripping both pieces of wood. Put the work aside until the glue has set.

FIG. 17. "BARBOLA" EDGED COVER.
CUT OUT OVER CIMBAL SIDES

FIG. 18. TURNING THE EDGE.

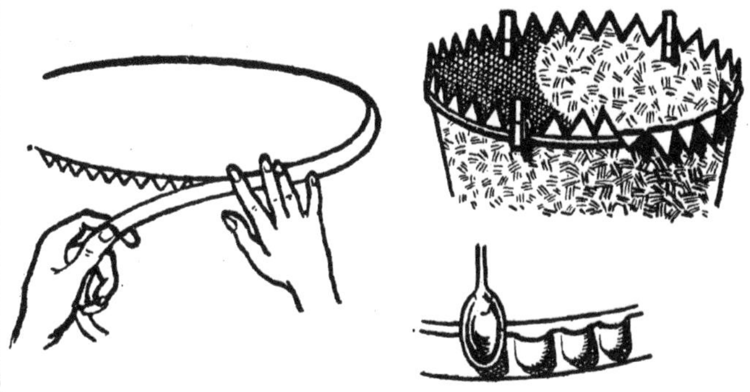

When the vertical join is hard and firm, the cover should be attached to the foundation frame. To do this, place the cover inside the rings—use clothes pegs to hold the rings in place and fold the edges of the parchment over the rings on the *outside* of the cover—treat the material gently, and re-position the pegs to hold the folded edge (see Fig. 18). With strong cotton threaded through a medium-fine needle, stitch through the folded edge and the cover, as near the rings as possible. Make the stitches neat and even, for although they will not be seen from the outside, being covered by the modelled edge, they may be visible on the inside of the cover. Stitch firmly and secure both ends of the cover over the wire ring. After the cover has been assembled on the rings of the frame, the modelled edge may be fitted and worked.

The modelled **"Barbola"** edge can be any width to suit the requirements of the lampshade maker, but the width should be suitable for the size of the lampshade. A rim of modelled **"Barbola"** about one half to three-quarters of an inch would be suitable for the lampshade illustrated. To make the modelled edge, first mark a pencil line round the top and bottom of the cover, near the folded edges, to the width of the modelled edge. Take some **"Barbola" Paste,** place it on a smooth surface, such as a piece of glass, and roll it to a thin sheet with a piece of smooth round wood. If the **"Barbola" Paste** sticks to the wood, hands or glass, a dusting of **"Gesso"** powder will prevent that. Roll the paste thinly, then cut it in strips to the width of the modelled edge. The strips are applied to the parchment, but to ensure fast adherence, it is necessary to brush liquid glue on the parchment before attaching the strips of paste. Apply glue to the area to be covered, and position the strip of **"Barbola" Paste** over the glued surface of the material, as illustrated in Fig. 18. Continue working round the lampshade cover at the top and bottom edges. Then with a boxwood modelling tool, smooth over the joins of the strips of paste and neaten the edges of the strips. The smooth strips of **"Barbola" Paste** can be modelled with any tool that will mark the plastic material, and any pattern required, can be worked. In Fig. 18, a spoon is illustrated marking the paste—this is rather like modelling the edge of a pastry pie cover.

After modelling the bands of **"Barbola" Paste,** the material should be allowed to harden and may then be coloured. **Winsor & Newton's Scholastic Water Colours** are ideal for colouring **"Barbola"**. After colouring, the outside of the lampshade—parchment cover and modelled edge—should be given a coat of clear varnish.

If parchment lampshade covers are to be decorated by painting them, the decoration is best applied before the cover is fixed to the frame.

CHAPTER VII

Different treatment of materials — a craft of invention — use of two materials — novel form of decoration — preparation — pattern making — cutting thonging holes — decorating the inner cover — assembling the cover — variation of decoration. **A stencil-cut Parchment Cover:** Preparation and shaping the cover — 'ties' in cutting designs — cutting the designs — glueing the vertical joins — attaching the two-part cover — variety in treatment. **A Novelty frameless lampshade:** Ingenious treatment — strip cover — heat-sealing ends and edges — washer reinforcement — fitting to a base. **" Crinothene " covers for tube lighting:** Frames — construction — future developments. **Cylindrical Lampshade:** Dimensions — wood base — batten-holder — pattern and cutting — assembling — finishing. **A Nursery Lampshade:** Rotating inside cover — gimbal adaptor — details of construction — metal top piece — assembling the rotating cover — fitting and adjustment.

SKILL in shaping and manipulating materials is not the only contribution to craftsmanship in lampshade making. It is necessary also, to fully consider the possibilities of materials and their properties, in the application of original design and treatment. This chapter describes the making of lampshades which may almost be described as 'novelties', and the inclusion of the descriptions given is to demonstrate different uses of materials, which are sometimes regarded as having only limited applications. Lampshade making is a craft of invention, and providing new ideas are not too revolutionary, there is no reason why conventional designs and treatment should be rigidly adhered to. It is not suggested that all the lampshades described in this chapter will appeal to everyone, but the object of these instructions is to present ideas which may be adapted and improved upon by the worker with imagination.

The first lampshade described is illustrated in Fig. 19. The foundation frame has a square top and base, and curved side-members are fitted at the corners to make the sides concave. The cover is made from two different materials, which permit the inclusion of a novel form of decoration. The outer cover of the lampshade can be of a translucent material, and the inside covering material is transparent. Silhouetted shapes are painted on the inside covering material, which spring into being when the shade is used over a lighted lamp, but which cannot be seen when the lamp is not lighted. For

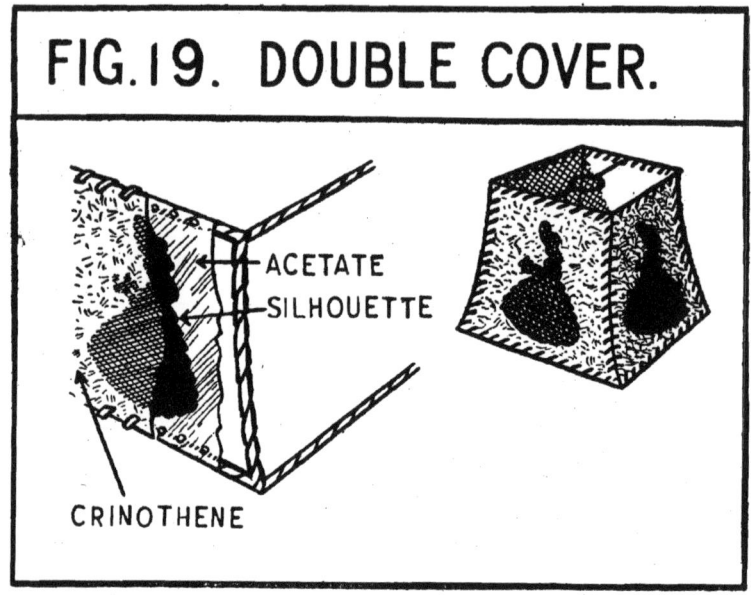

FIG. 19. DOUBLE COVER.
ACETATE
SILHOUETTE
CRINOTHENE

this particular lampshade, the material described is **"Crinothene"** which is ivory in colour, and the cover is thonged to the foundation frame.

Prepare the frame in the usual way, by checking it for faults, etc., and binding it with bias binding of a light cream or white, to match the covering material. After binding the frame, make a pattern for the side panels. As the pattern is to be used several times, it should be cut in card. Mark the pattern to shape, by placing it on something resilient, and pressing the frame against the card, marking with a pencil. Cut the card pattern accurately to shape, and check it against all the sides of the lampshade. Mark out and cut four pieces of ivory **"Crinothene"** for the outer cover, and four pieces of transparent or frosted acetate for the inside cover. If any of the side panels are different in size, pair the **"Crinothene"** and acetate, for attachment to particular sides. After cutting the cover pieces, neatly and accurately to shape, thonging holes should be punched. The distances between the holes and from the edges of the panels is explained and illustrated in a previous chapter. When cutting holes in the panels, clip the paired panel materials together with strong paper-clips or clothes pegs, and make certain that the same number of holes are punched in each of the upright edges of adjoining panels. After punching the holes, which should be large enough to permit easy passage of the thonging material without placing undue strain on the edges of the panels, the panels may be decorated and assembled.

A suitable decoration should be painted on the acetate panels. This may take any form to suit the requirements of the worker. In the shade illustrated, a simple Victorian silhouette is used. Make a drawing or tracing of the decoration and place it under the acetate panel. Use oil colours or spirit colours, and neatly paint the design. It may be done in black only, or if the design is composed of large coloured sections, these may be coloured on the acetate. The painted side of the acetate is placed against the inside of the **"Crinothene"** when the shade is assembled, so make certain that the decoration ss painted on the right side of the material. Decorate the four panels of acetate, not forgetting to keep them paired with the outside panels. Allow the paint to dry before assembling the cover.

When the paint has dried, the cover may be thonged to the foundation frame. Take a piece of thonging and attach one end of it to the frame, at the top edge near one of the corners. Take two adjoining panels, place the two parts of each panel together and clip them to the frame with pegs or paper-clips. Thong down the corner of the lampshade, pulling the thonging just tight enough to hold the panels in place, work down to the bottom of the curved side member, cut the thonging and tuck the end neatly away inside the lampshade. Fasten the top of the thonging in the same way. Attach the next panel, clip it to the frame and thong down the curved side-member at the corner. Fasten off the ends of the thonging neatly and firmly, and attach the remaining panel and thong it to the frame. Work round the top edge of the lampshade next with thonging, then finish with the bottom edge.

This type of lampshade is particularly attractive in certain settings, and the form of decoration may be executed to suit the room in which the lampshade is to be used. For instance, a lampshade for use in a nursery could be decorated with animals and fairies or fairy tale characters. Transfers may be used instead of painting the decoration, or feathers may be affixed between the two panels, or leaves or cut paper shapes and, of course, the method may be applied to lampshade frames of different shapes to the one illustrated.

A simple Empire-type lampshade frame is used as the foundation of the next shade described, which is illustrated in Fig. 20. The cover is a double one, and may be made from one kind of material only—such as parchment—or two different materials may be used—say parchment and acetate. Parchment paper is perhaps the most suitable form of covering and for this double cover, thin material should be used (parchment paper is available in a variety of thicknesses). The decorative design is cut in the outside cover rather like a stencil, but the material itself is not stencilled.

To make the lampshade, first inspect the frame and cover

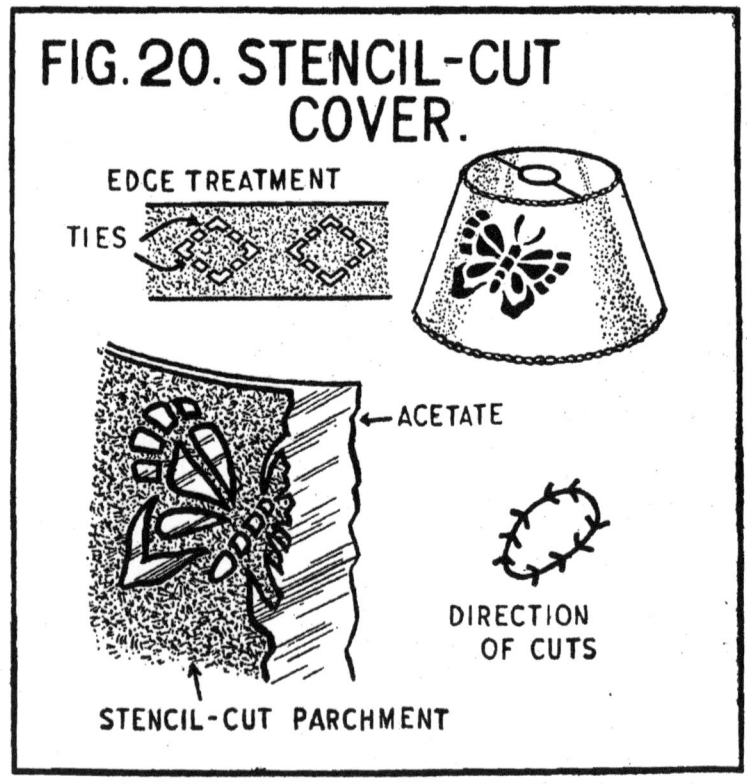

FIG. 20. STENCIL-CUT COVER.

it with bias binding of a suitable colour. Make a pattern (previously described and illustrated in detail), in thin card, and mark round it with pencil on the parchment. Cut two covers in thin material, and when using pencil on parchment, remember that it is not very easy to remove pencil lines, so do not make any unnecessary pencil marks on the material. Make allowance for the ends of the covers to overlap, and cut both parchment shapes to the same size. The lampshade cover described is stitched to the foundation frame, so it will not be necessary to cut holes for thonging, unless that method of attaching is preferred by the worker. After cutting the covers to shape, test them on the frame, and when testing the parchment covers for fit, place them together with the vertical seams opposite to each other. One of the covers does not need attention until it is fitted to the frame, but the other cover requires treatment to effect the decoration.

To decorate the cover, draw a suitable decoration on the pattern. Use pencil and mark the lines of the decoration boldly. The decoration may take the form of a simple pierced edge at top and bottom of the cover (see Fig. 20), or it may be more elaborate. The treatment of the decoration should be the same as the method used for cutting stencils, and it should be remembered that 'ties' will be necessary to hold some parts of the design together—use of 'ties' is illustrated in Fig. 20. However, whatever design is selected, the outlines should be marked boldly on the pattern originally made. When the design has been completely outlined, the outside cover should be placed over the pattern and the outlines traced on the parchment with fine pencil lines. Parchment is a translucent material, and when placed close to the original design on the pattern, the pencil lines should be clearly visible through the parchment. Be careful when marking the parchment not to make any unnecessary pencil marks, which may be found difficult to remove. The next part of the work is to cut through the pencil lines, so that the design is pierced through the material. A very sharp stencil knife will be required, or a penknife which has been well sharpened and shaped to a point. To cut the material, place it on a piece of stout card or glass, but best of all on zinc, and work through the pencilled outlines with the point of the knife. When cutting, always work away from corners (as illustrated in Fig. 20), to avoid over-cutting into the material. When cutting curves, the material may be moved as the knife is drawn through the parchment. Cut the surplus material out neatly and cleanly, and the shade is ready to be assembled.

The vertical seams of the covers should be joined first with liquid glue, as previously described, and the seams should be arranged so that they are opposite each other in the cover. The edges at the top and bottom of the cover may also be glued, but only a small amount of glue is required. As the cover is to be stitched to the foundation frame, it would be advisable to punch stitch holes through the material, before sewing, and this should be done before the covers are fastened together. The pierced cover should be fitted outside. When the glue has dried, the cover may be sewn to the foundation frame. Use strong cotton for sewing, threaded through a medium-fine needle, and stitch through both covers firmly, securing them to the frame binding. Be careful not to pull the cotton too tight, or it may break through the edges of the material. After sewing the cover to the frame, gimp or braid of suitable colour can be attached. This may be sewn or glued to the cover, and should be arranged to conceal the edges of the material.

These stencil-cut lampshades are quite easy to make and the method of decoration is very effective when the lamp over which the shade is mounted, is lighted. There is great scope for variety in treatment, and the method is not restricted to Empire shapes. There is one important thing to remember when sticking gimp or braid to lampshade covers. The adhesive or cement used must be suitable, and this is particularly important when cementing fabrics to plastic covering materials. Generally, it is more satisfactory if the braids are stitched.

Our next lampshade is really a novelty lampshade, and is included to demonstrate how conventional designs may be broken away from, if the material is suitable for the purpose. It is not suggested that the type of cover described is perfect in design or is preferred over other types. The intention is, to demonstrate ingenuity and originality in treatment. The lampshade is illustrated in Fig. 21. It is roughly globular in shape and is made of **"Crinothene"**—the chief feature of the lampshade is that it is not made over a foundation frame. Obviously a lampshade of this type would have to be a small one, and to provide extra strength, the one described has a cover of double **"Crinothene"**.

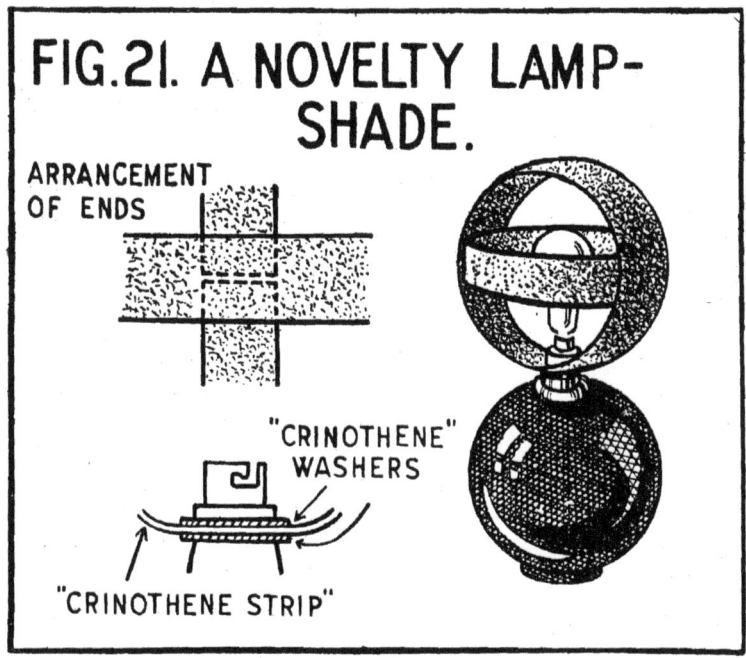

FIG. 21. A NOVELTY LAMPSHADE.

A pattern should be made for this unusual lampshade, and it should be of thin cardboard. It is in the form of two strips of thin cardboard, which can be made any length or width to suit a particular requirement, but the width of the strips should not exceed two and a half inches, although they may be narrower, if required. Cut two strips of cardboard to the width decided, and make them into an open roll, one roll should be formed over the other, and the roughly assembled shape tried for size on a suitable base. After adjustment as necessary, the pattern pieces may be used for marking the material to size and shape. There is one important point to consider. The openings between the bands of **"Crinothene"** should be large enough to permit the insertion of an electric lamp bulb for fitting into the lamp-holder socket. Four pieces of the covering material are required, and the outside pieces should be a little longer than the inner pieces, to take up the extra thickness of the material. The lampshade is heat-sealed to hold the parts together, with the ends of the material so arranged as to provide maximum strength and neatness.

To assemble the lampshade, take the inside pieces of the cover and place them together, so that the ends are arranged as illustrated in Fig. 21. Clip the two pieces together or pin them to a wood support. Heat an electric soldering iron and heat-seal the joining edges on both sides, taking care that the iron is heated to a temperature only sufficient to soften and seal the **"Crinothene"**. After jointing the two inner strips, take the two outer strips of **"Crinothene"** and fasten them over the shaped inside of the lampshade, holding them in position with strong clips. Arrange the ends of the outside strips at the other side of the shape to the ends of the inner strips, and in opposite order of joining to those of the first strips. Heat-seal the ends of the outer strips of the cover. After assembling the four strips of material, and firmly joining the ends, the edges of the strips should be sealed, and this is best done by heating a knife blade and smoothing it at right angles over the edges of the strips of **"Crinothene"**. A little practise on some odd scraps will indicate how effective this method is. After sealing all the edges, a hole should be cut where the ends of the strips are joined on the outside of the shape. The hole should be cleanly cut, and should be made large enough to fit over the bulb-holder socket. This hole should be strengthened by cutting a **"Crinothene"** washer about a quarter inch thick all round, and heat-sealing it round the hole. The lampshade is held in position by fitting the reinforced hole over the lamp-holder socket and screwing the retaining ring in place. This novel lampshade is quite easy to make, and although it is not intended to replace shades of a more conventional design and construction, it can be most effectively used in certain settings.

"Crinothene" is an ideal material for covering fluorescent lighting tubes. The cover will not sag, nor be affected by heat, if it is fitted three inches or more from the tube wall. It will be necessary to make a wood or metal frame to hold the **"Crinothene"** in place over the light tube, according to the type of lighting used. The illustrations in Fig. 22 show two simple types of fittings suitable for use with wall lights or ceiling lights. Really, the construction of lampshades for tubular lighting depends on the ingenuity of the individual worker, and the two methods illustrated are offered as suggestions only. Fluorescent lighting is still quite a new thing

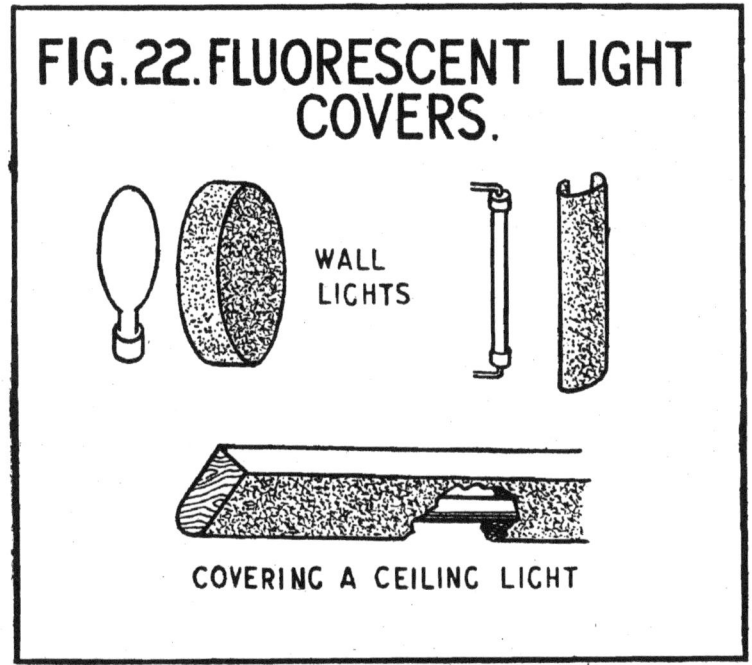

FIG. 22. FLUORESCENT LIGHT COVERS.

WALL LIGHTS

COVERING A CEILING LIGHT

and, no doubt, there will be developments, and many shapes and forms of lighting fittings and tubes will be produced.

"**Crinothene**" is a very adaptable material, and the next lampshade described demonstrates effective use for the material in a rather unusual way. The lampshade is illustrated in Fig. 23, and consists of a cylindrical shade. The top and base of the shade are four inches in diameter and seven inches in height. It is a table model and no base of any kind is used, although a fitting for the lamp-holder socket is fixed inside the cover. Only one ring is required for the top of the lampshade. The bottom is fitted round the wood support for the lamp-holder socket.

To make the lampshade (the dimensions may be altered if desired), first shape a piece of wood. The wood should be about one inch thick, and circular. All sides and edges should be rubbed smooth with glasspaper. Attach a batten socket fitting to the circular piece of wood, as illustrated in Fig. 23. A hole should be drilled in the centre of the wood mount before fixing the batten socket in place, and a groove cut in

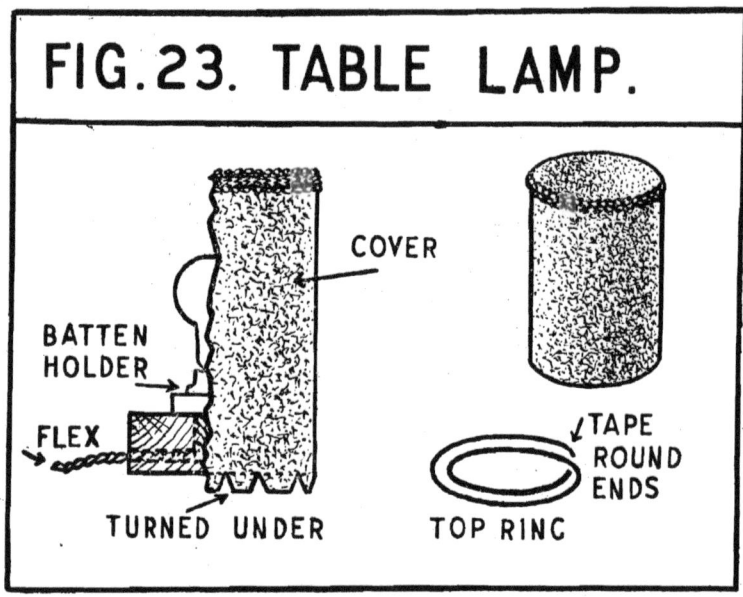

the underside of the wood from the central hole to the edge, large enough to hold the flex. A wire ring, the same size as the wooden piece, should be obtained, or made. To make a small ring, cut a piece of wire (about half the thickness of lampshade wire), twice the length required, shape it round a tin, and bind it with adhesive tape as illustrated in Fig. 23. Make a pattern for the cover from a piece of stout cardboard, and mark out and cut the **"Crinothene"** cover. Allow an extra half an inch at the bottom of the cover for turning under the wood base. Cut V-notches in the bottom edge of the cover, then heat-seal the vertical join. Overlap the edges of the **"Crinothene"** at the vertical join, seal them strongly with a heated iron and with a small heated tool, model the join to the same pattern as the **"Crinothene"** surface. Bind the top ring of the frame with bias binding of a suitable colour. Place the small ring in the top of the cover and stitch through the material and frame binding. Sew a narrow gimp round the top of the cover and round the bottom of the cover, level with the inside ends of the V-notches. Carefully fit the cover over the wood base, fold the bottom edges of the **"Crinothene"** under the wood base and fasten them to the wood with short nails with fairly large heads. To complete the lamp, cut a piece of felt to fit under the base and glue it in place to the wood. Care should be taken when finishing the bottom of the lamp not to fill the groove cut in the wood base with the felt.

The lampshades described in this chapter have been included to demonstrate fresh applications of materials. There is no limit to the scope of the home lampshade maker, providing that ingenuity and imagination are exercised. It is not suggested that conventional shapes and designs be ignored, but rather that they should not be considered as restrictive. The craft is one of invention, and this should be remembered.

The final lampshade described in this chapter of novel lampshades is a nursery shade. It may also be used for advertising purposes. The cover is made in two separate parts, one of which rotates inside the other by means of hot air rotating a vane at the top of the inner cover. The inside rotating cover should be suitably decorated so that the silhouette shadow of the decoration is thrown on the outside cover. A cylindrical or Empire lampshade is suitable for use as an outer cover. The Empire foundation frame should have a gimbal ring fitted to the top member of the frame, and a gimbal adaptor should be used to convert the pendant lampshade to a table type, and also support the rotating inner cover. The lampshade is illustrated in Fig. 24, with part of the shade covering omitted, to show how the inside is constructed. The outer cover should be made in the way previously described, and parchment or translucent acetate should be used as the covering material.

The rotating inner cover should be made from transparent acetate with a thin metal circular top. The acetate is shaped and fitted to the metal top which is slotted and the material bent to form vanes. The rotating inner piece should be suspended from the gimbal adaptor to fit over the electric lamp. If necessary, the side supports of the gimbal adaptor should be bent to allow room for the rotating acetate cover. When fitting the metal and acetate cover over the lamp, care should be taken to ensure that it will move freely on the bearing. The heated air rising from the lighted lamp is sufficient to move the vanes in the metal top, and the inner part of the cover will move round under its own power for as long as the lamp is alight.

To make the inner cover, cut a circular piece of thin metal with a diameter of approximately three and three quarter

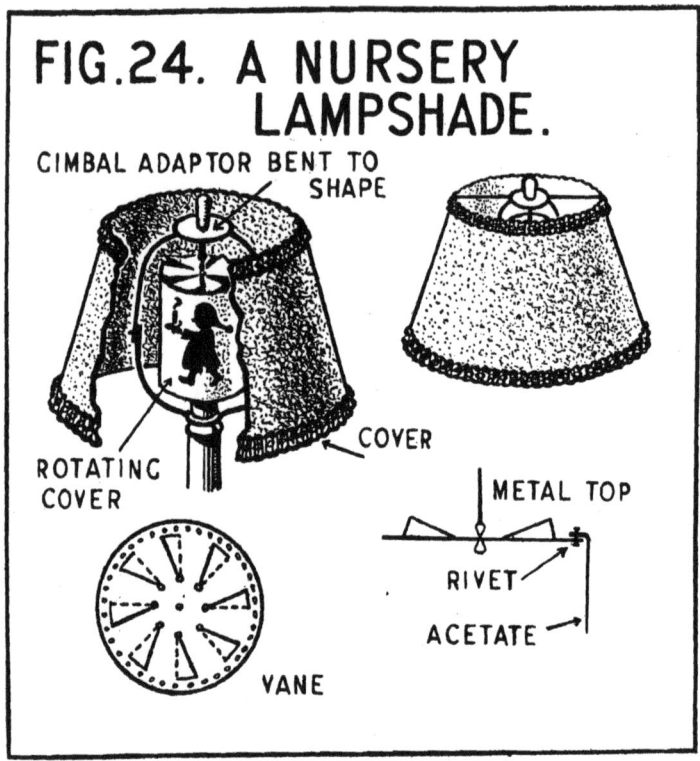

Fig. 24. A Nursery Lampshade.

inches. Drill holes in the top and cut slits from the holes to the edges of the top, as illustrated in Fig. 24. With a sharp-pointed bradawl, punch holes round the edge of the shaped top. Cut a piece of acetate about four inches wide and long enough to fit round the metal vane, and cut V-notches in the top of the acetate to fold over the metal top. Small rivets are used to secure the acetate to the metal rotating top as illustrated in Fig. 24, and the overlapping edges should be joined with acetate adhesive. Use a piece of wire bent to shape to hang the inner cover from the gimbal adaptor, and paint suitable designs on the outside of the acetate. Care should be taken to ensure that the acetate rotating cover will move freely on the bearing, and some adjustment may be necessary of the bearing and the pitch of the vanes, when the lampshade is assembled.

CHAPTER VIII

Lampshade bases: Aid to sales — use of common articles and objects — converting a vase — plug for the neck — suitable materials — shaping the plug — care in fitting — attaching the socket — another pottery base — different conversion treatment — use of back plates — drilling pottery and glass — suitable lubricant — practise — assembling the lamp base. A covered bottle — pattern — use of "**Crinothene**" — thonged corners — finishing — assembling — light reflection. A preserve jar with moulded cover — use of "**Wallart**" — mixing and applying — drying — final coat — stippled finish — insulating the flex hole. A candlestick lamp base made from "**Crinothene**" — fittings — making the column — heat-sealed edges — making the base — handle — wiring-up and fitting — a cord-covered base — suitable foundation — attaching the cord — decorative treatment.

QUITE a large proportion of lampshades made are for use on table lamps, and the home craftsman working for profit will appreciate that there is greater chance of sales if lampshade stands and bases are made and offered with the shades. This chapter, therefore, deals with some of the methods of making and fitting bases. A great many common articles can be utilised for lampshade bases. Such things as vases, bottles, jars, leap to mind, and if the approach to their transformation is imaginative and ingenious, these simple objects may be made worth many times their cost.

The first lampshade stand described and illustrated in Fig. 25 is a pottery vase of simple design. To make vases of this type into lampshade bases, it is necessary to fit a lamp-holder socket to the top of the article. For a vase with a wide neck, such as the one illustrated, the socket fitting may be attached to a piece of wood or cork cut to shape, to fit into the mouth of the vase. Tackle the job in the following sequence.

The materials required are a piece of wood or cork about an inch thick, a batten socket (as illustrated), to hold the lamp bulb, three one-inch screws to fit the socket to the top, some flex of suitable colour, and a torpedo switch for fitting over the flex (if desired, the switch may be incorporated in the lamp-holder socket, but the batten type sockets described are not often fitted with press switches). In addition, some strong liquid glue will be required, a pair of scissors and a screwdriver.

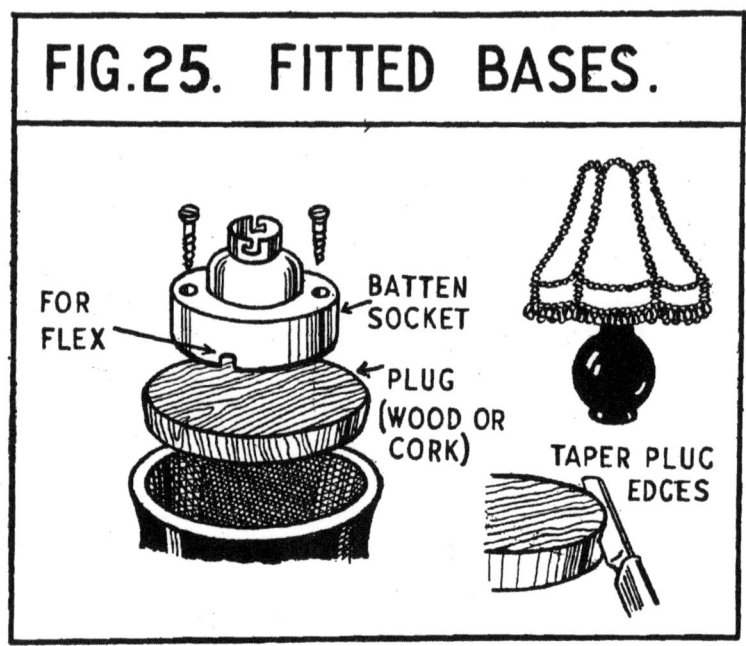

FIG. 25. FITTED BASES.

The first thing to do is to cut the piece of wood or cork to shape, to fit firmly into the top of the vase. This should be done carefully as it is very easy to crack the top of a vase, if too much force is used. It is best to taper-trim the edges of the material with a very sharp knife (see Fig. 25), and finish off with glass-paper. Before fitting the shaped plug in the top of the vase, the batten socket should be attached to it. If the plug is made of wood, it is a simple matter to screw the socket into place, but if it is made of cork, it may be found that the screws may not hold very well, and if that is so, longer screws should be used through the cork and fastened into a piece of wood placed under the top—this is illustrated in Fig. 25. Before attaching the socket fitting, provision should be made for the flex. This may be fitted at the top of the plug, by removing a small piece of the side of the fitting at the bottom, or it may be fitted through a hole in the plug and brought up through another hole in the side of the plug (see the illustration). When the batten-holder has been firmly fixed in place and flex fitted, if it has to go through the top, the shaped piece should be fitted to the top of the vase. Brush liquid glue round the edge of the shaped top and inside the top of the vase. Insert the shaped top in the vase, making certain that it is firmly housed, and set the base aside for the glue to set. The lamp should be wired up after the glue has set, and the top of the plug should be treated to tone with the lampshade base. If it is considered necessary to weight the base, this should be done before fixing the top in place. Sand is suitable for weighting lampshade bases.

The next lampshade base described is also made from a pottery vase, but the conversion treatment is different from that of the first vase. The lamp socket of this lamp-base, which is illustrated in Fig. 26, incorporates a press switch, the top of the vase is smaller, and the flex is fitted through a hole drilled in the side of the vase at the bottom. First a wood or cork plug should be made to fit into the top of the vase. It should be made to fit into the top of the vase. It should fit snugly with tapered edges, and should not require any force to insert it. A hole for the flex should be drilled through the middle of the plug, and a back plate—illustrated in Fig. 26—should be fitted directly over the drilled hole. The flat base of the back plate is drilled for screwing, and it should be fitted firmly to the plug. The top of the back plate is threaded, to take the lamp-holder socket. After preparing the top, and before it is glued in place, a hole should be drilled through the pottery vase. Drilling through pottery or glass is not very difficult, providing care is taken, but it is advisable to practise first on odd pieces of pottery and glass before attempting to make a hole in a valuable piece.

A very hard drill is required for drilling glass and pottery and it should be used with a lubricant made by shredding camphor in turpentine. Before drilling, wrap a piece of cloth round the vase or bottle, and fix it carefully in a vice, or get someone to hold it for you. Mark the position of the hole, which may be started with the point of a broken file, and commence drilling. Use a high speed drill and do not exert too much pressure on the article being drilled. Use the lubricant freely and hold the drill very lightly, when it is apparent that it is about to come through the other side of the material. After drilling practise holes in odd pieces of material, the worker should have acquired the 'feel' of the operation, and be able to work on valuable pieces. After drilling the base,

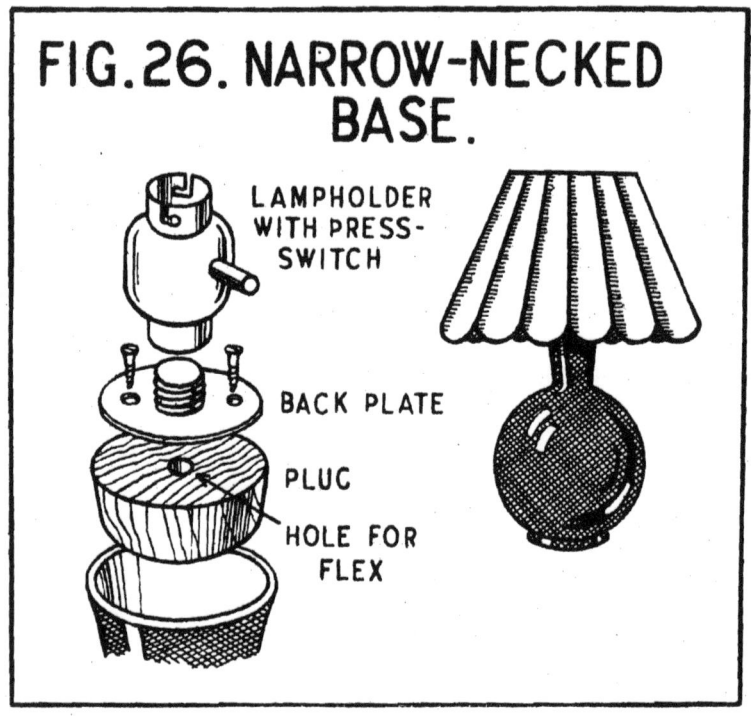

FIG. 26. NARROW-NECKED BASE.

the lamp may be assembled; thread one end of a length of flex through the drilled hole and bring it out through the top of the vase. Thread the end through the hole in the plug and, leaving some to spare for fitting to the socket, tie a single knot to hold the flex in place. Brush glue round the tapered edge of the plug and inside the top of the vase, insert the plug and leave it to firmly set.

When the glue has set, untie the knot in the top end of the flex and wire-up the combination press-switch lampsocket, and screw it over the back plate. At the other end of the flex, fit a suitable electric plug. The top of the vase plug should be treated, to merge it with the colour and texture of the vase. If it is thought necessary to weight the base, it should be done before the shaped plug of wood or cork is affixed inside the top of the vase. Sand is usually used for weighting lampshade bases, but in the case of a drilled base, where the sand would be likely to trickle through the hole, some other weighting material should be used. Plaster is suitable, providing a passage is left for the flex. Flex is obtainable in many colour finishes, and a suitable coloured flex should be used with lamp bases, to tone with the general colour scheme.

In Fig. 27, another type of lampshade base is shown. It is made from a bottle with square corners, which is covered with **"Crinothene"** of the same colour, or a contrasting colour to that of the lampshade cover of the same material. All kinds of bottles may be covered in this way, even if the manufacturer's name is embossed on the side of the bottle. To make a **"Crinothene"** cover for a bottle base, a pattern should first be made in stiff card. Place the bottle on a sheet of thin card, mark round the base with a pencil, and from the corners, draw pencil lines as shown in the illustration. Cut and remove the waste card and test the pattern over the bottle (see Fig. 27). The corner edges of the pattern should meet. Shape the top of the pattern to the neck of the bottle, and,

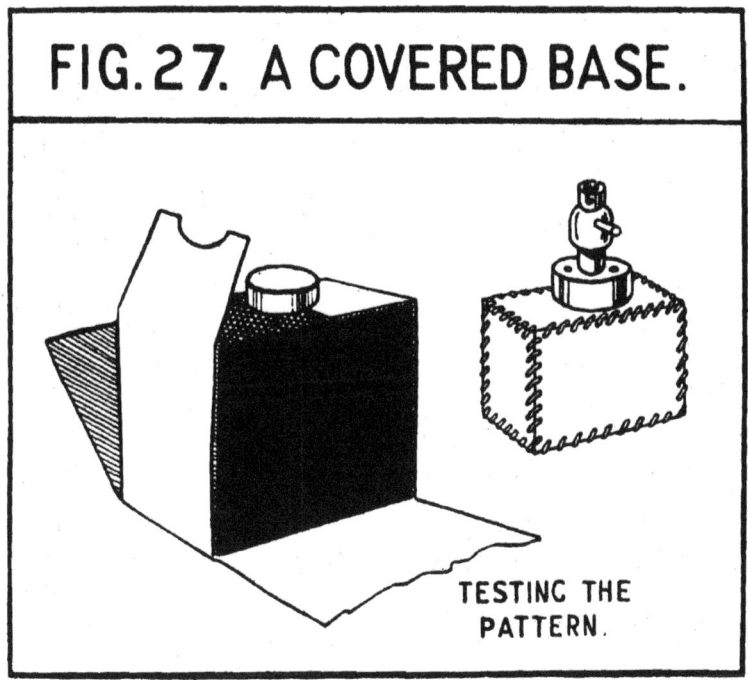

FIG. 27. A COVERED BASE.

TESTING THE PATTERN.

when it is a perfect fit, use it for marking and cutting the **"Crinothene"** to shape. After cutting the cover to shape, punch thonging holes in each of the joining edges and make certain that the same number of holes are punched in each pair of joining edges. Drill a hole through the bottle, near the base in one side, then attach the cover. Place the bottle over the **"Crinothene"** shape and bend the sides of the material up to cover the bottle. Wind string round the sides of the cover near the top to hold it firm while thonging, and commence thonging the corners of the cover. Begin from the bottom of the corners, thong one or two holes, joining one corner, then commence fastening the other corners. Thong upwards and fasten one or two holes in each corner of the base-cover in turn. Fasten the neck firmly, knot the ends of the thonging and neatly tuck the odd ends of thonging between the cover and the glass. Cut a small hole in the cover where the glass has been drilled to permit passage of the flex, which should be of a colour to match or tone with the colour of the **"Crinothene"**. After completing the cover, a back plate should be fitted to the metal screw-top closure of the jar. First pierce a hole for the flex in the centre of the top of the screw top of the bottle, remove any paint from the cap of the bottle, and solder the base of the metal back plate to the closure, making sure that the hole in the back plate is over the hole in the top of the cap. Paint the cap and the back plate to match the cover, but be careful not to clog the threads of the top of the back plate with too thick a coat of paint. After fitting the back plate, and wiring the flex to a combined switch socket-holder, which should be screwed over the back plate, the lamp is ready for use. If the jar used for the base has a fairly wide bottom, it should not be necessary to weight it, and the light from the lamp will shine into the **"Crinothene"** covered glass base, giving it a very pleasing appearance when in use.

Many other types and shapes of bottles and jars are suitable for use as lamp bases. In Fig. 28, is illustrated a preserve jar used as a foundation on which to shape a lamp-base for a bedside lamp. The material used for covering the jar is **"Wallart"**, a **Winsor & Newton** product. **"Wallart"** is a white powder which, when mixed with water, forms a paste. The paste may be modelled, carved and moulded to any shape required, and is used extensively in the decoration of walls for stippled or modelled finishes. To make a lamp-base

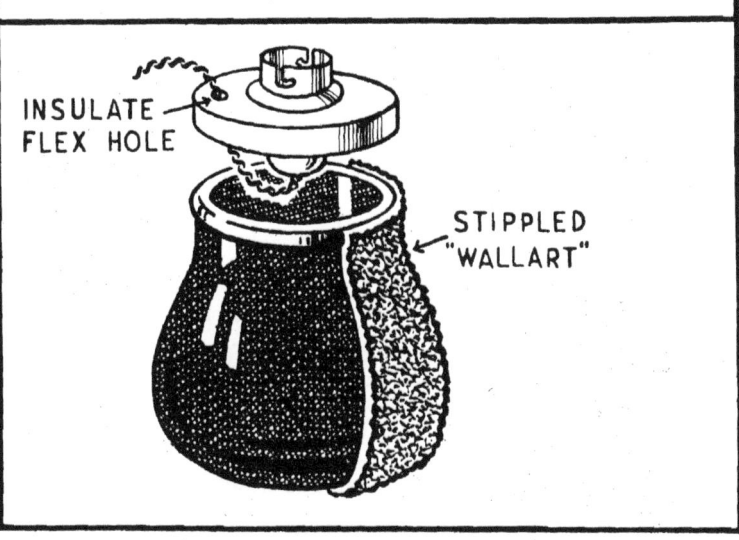

FIG. 28. CONVERTED BASE.

of the type illustrated, clean the jar and remove the cap. Mix **"Wallart"** with water, adding the powder to the water (full instructions are given on the packet), and spread the paste which should be mixed rather thickly, over the jar. With a broad knife or modelling tool, roughly shape the **"Wallart"** covering. Put the covered jar aside until the **"Wallart"** has hardened, and do not try to accelerate hardening by the application of heat. When the **"Wallart"** has set and is hard, it may be rubbed down with coarse glasspaper, or a coarse file, to shape. After shaping, any dust should be removed by brushing, and another coat of **"Wallart"** applied. The second coat, which is also the final coat, should not be mixed so thickly as the first coat. Apply the final coat of **"Wallart"** and stipple it. This may be done with a sponge or a stiff brush, which should be lightly tapped all over the material, while it is soft. After stippling, set the lamp-base aside for the covering to harden. When it is hard and dry, it may be coloured. A coat of size should be applied first and then the stippled cover may be painted with oil colours, being finally

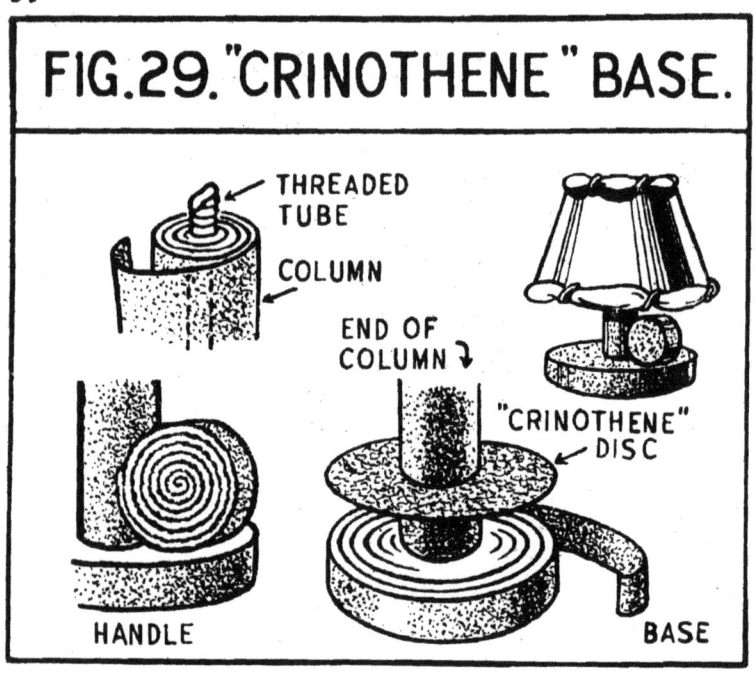

FIG. 29. "CRINOTHENE" BASE.

varnished. **"Wallart"** is a very useful material and may be used for many craftwork purposes. A lamp-holder should be fitted to the closure of the jar, as illustrated in Fig. 28, by cutting a hole in the metal top large enough for entry of the lamp-holder socket, which is kept in place by screwing the two parts of the socket together over the cap. A smaller hole should be cut in the metal top of the jar for the flex, and an insulating washer should be fitted, to prevent the flex becoming frayed in contact with the edges of the hole. After assembly and wiring-up, the lamp is ready for use.

"Crinothene" may be used for making lamp-bases without the addition of any other material, except the fitting. A solid **"Crinothene"** lamp-base is illustrated in Fig. 29. It is shaped in the form of a candle and candle-stick, and is quite easy to make. A metal tube is required, upon which the upright column is formed, and the tube should be threaded at one end to take a bulb-holder socket. The base may be made any size, but it would be better to make it small, rather than large, which would be out of character with the design. To make this attractive lamp-base, first obtain a five and a half inch length of tubing with a screw thread cut in one end for attachment of the bulb socket. Cut "Crinothene" in strips, five and a half inches wide, and for this, odd pieces may be used up, providing they are all the same colour. The strips of "Crinothene" should be tightly rolled round the column support, leaving the threaded end of the tube to project at one end for about half an inch, with a recess at the other end of the roll to make a passage for the flex. Roll the strips round tightly and heat-seal the joins if odd lengths of the material are used. Make the column to a thickness of about one-and-a-quarter inches in diameter, and heat-seal the overlapping end of the "Crinothene" on the outside of the roll, marking it with a small heated tool to resemble the roughened surface of the material, and heat-seal the top and bottom edges of the column. Cut a "Crinothene" circle with a hole in it large enough to cover the top of the column completely (see the illustration—Fig. 29), place it over the top of the column and heat-seal the edges of the holed disc to the round edge at the top of the roll forming the column. Use the heated blade of a small knife and model the edges of the material carefully.

The base of the lamp-stand is made next and is also formed of strips of "Crinothene". These may be cut from odd pieces of material and should be from three-quarters of an inch to one inch wide. Heat-seal the end of the first strip to the base of the column and wind it round. Heat-seal all joining edges and continue rolling the narrow strips round the base of the column until it measures four-and-a-half to five inches across the base. Carefully heat-seal the final end of the roll and model it with a tool to resemble the roughened surface of "Crinothene". Drill horizontally through the roll from the outside of the base to the recessed centre of the base, for the passage of flex, which is fitted after completing the lamp-base. With a broad-bladed knife, which should be heated, smooth over the underside of the circular base, joining the edges of the material and making the base smooth and even. Cut a round piece of "Crinothene", with a hole in the centre to fit over the column and use it to cover the top of the base. With a small heated knife, heat-seal the outside edge of this piece, to the top edge of the circular base and model the edges to conceal the join. The ring handle shown in the illustration—

Fig. 29, is built up of strips of **"Crinothene"**, heat-sealed to the column and base, and with edges heat-sealed and covered with round pieces of **"Crinothene"**. Care should be taken at every stage to ensure that the heat-sealed joints are strongly made. After making the base, it should be wired up, using flex of a suitable colour, and a press-switch socket-holder screwed over the top of the column. Many different shapes and styles of lampshades may be made by shaping and heat-sealing **"Crinothene"**, and the lampshades used with them covered with the same material, in the same colour, or a contrasting colour.

"Perspex" is suitable for use with **"Crinothene"** and other materials, for making stands and bases for lampshades, providing the material is used intelligently and the design and colouring is suitable. Many other articles and materials may be used, and the home worker will find that sales are more readily effected, if table lamps and bases are offered together. The final lamp-base described illustrates the use of a very simple material.

An ordinary jam jar with a metal closure forms the foundation of the base, which is illustrated in Fig. 30, and

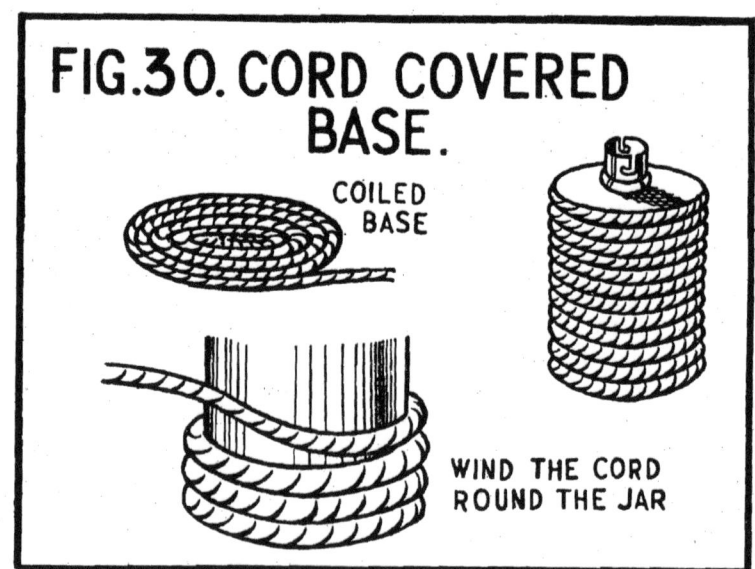

FIG. 30. CORD COVERED BASE.
COILED BASE
WIND THE CORD ROUND THE JAR

over which, sash cord is fastened. The cord is first coiled round itself to form the bottom of the lamp base, and is secured with a suitable adhesive. The cord is wound round the jar, using an adhesive on the winding and glass, to hold the cover in place, and fastened off neatly at the top of the jar, leaving room for metal snap-cap (to which a socket is fitted) to be attached. After the adhesive has set, and the base can be handled, it should be singed all over with a lighted taper, to remove any short hairs sticking out from the cord. The cover may be left plain or painted. If it is painted, one or two coats of flat white undercoating should be applied first, finishing with a coat of gloss paint or enamel. The cord motif may be repeated on the cover of the lampshade, by trimming it with silk cord of a suitable colour.

CHAPTER IX

Decorating Lampshades: Suitable materials — applications — velvet — Ruching — description — stitching — drawing up — fastening off — Shell Ruching — diagonal stitching — finishing — Double Ruching — puffed ruching — Two-Colour Ruching — use of two ribbons — method — finishing. **Parchment:** Crackled 'antique' Parchment — imitation crackle effect — use of chemicals — small pattern — smoothing ridges — darkening cracks — finishing — practise — better method — necessity of plenty of practise — glue solution — applying the solution — liability to cockle — cracking in shrink-drying — avoidance of small pattern — darkening the cracks — finishing — emphasis on practise. **Painting on Parchment:** Suitable mediums — tracing the decorative design — degreasing the decoration area — changing colour values — fading of colours — use of transparent colours. **Decorative Thonging:** Suggestions — suitable leatherwork thonging stitches — silk cords. **Other Materials:** Use of lace — labels and stamps — a calendar lampshade cover — suitable Christmas gift — use of artificial flowers — " **Saree Relief Colours** " and metallic powders — applique — possibilities of the craft — assistance in obtaining supplies.

DECORATING lampshades has been generally dealt with in preceding chapters when describing shades of a particular style or type, but there is some extra information about decorating lampshades generally, which the beginner lampshade maker should know, and which is described in this final chapter.

It has been mentioned that many kinds of material may be used for edging and trimming, and this is particularly true of fabrics such as velvet, satin and cotton ribbons, and strips of covering materials, in addition to braids, gimps, cords, thonging, silk cords, etc. Attaching strips or ribbons of material should be done carefully and practice should be carried out with odd pieces of material before attempting the decoration of completed covers. Obviously the colour and texture of the material used for trimming, should be suitable for decorating the covering material, to match or contrast with the colourings. A favourite material for the decorative trimming of lampshades is velvet, which is suitable for use with most of the covering fabrics in matching, or preferably contrasting colour. The velvet may be stitched flat to the covering, or may be gathered in the form of 'ruching' which, for the benefit of beginners is explained in detail below.

Ruching: Is the term for gathering or rucking strips of material, and may be done by hand or by machine if an attachment is fitted. Ruching is illustrated in Fig. 31. The material is first stitched with a running stitch through the middle of the width and the full length of the strip. The cotton used should be very strong, and when the strip of material has been stitched along its length from end to end, the ends of the cotton should be pulled, to draw up and compress the strip of material along its length. If the stitching is done neatly, the gathers or tucks will be formed evenly. After drawing up the strip of material, the ends of the cotton should be firmly fastened, and the ruched ribbon or strip of material is then ready for sewing to the lampshade cover. This form of decoration is usually applied to edges rather than to upright seams.

Shell Ruching: This is done by stitching diagonally across and forward, through a strip of material, with running stitch, as illustrated in Fig. 31. After stitching the length of the material with strong cotton, the ends of the cotton should be

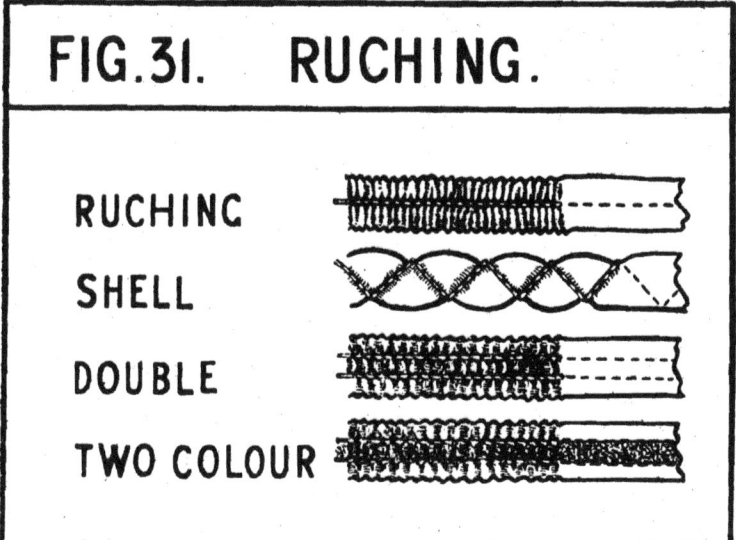

FIG. 31. RUCHING.

pulled, to draw up the material—see the illustration—and the ends of the cotton firmly fastened. The ruched ribbon or strip of material is then ready for attachment to the lampshade cover.

Double Ruching: Double ruching is done by sewing twice along the strip of material near the edges with strong cotton, forming a running stitch. When the ends of the cotton are pulled, to draw up the material, a particularly attractive puffed ruching is formed. After securing the ends of the cotton, the double ruched ribbon or strip of material may be sewn to the lampshade cover.

Two-colour Ruching: This is done by rucking two ribbons or strips of material of different widths as illustrated in Fig. 31. The narrow strip should be laid on the wide strip, and both should be stitched through, with a running stitch using strong cotton. Single or Shell ruching may be done with two coloured strips. After drawing up the material, the ends of the cotton should be firmly secured, before the ruched material is sewn to a lampshade cover.

Parchment is a material which lends itself readily to many forms of decoration. Stencilled designs may be applied, or the material may be painted with oil, water or spirit colours. Transfers may be used and a crackle finish may be applied to the surface of most kinds of parchment. The commercial method of 'crackling' parchment to simulate an antique appearance is a trade secret, but there are some simple methods for imitating this process, which may be practised by the home worker.

Crackled Antique Parchment: A simple method of imitating a crackled finish is with a fine pen and black ink to draw spidery lines on the material, varnishing over when the ink has dried. This is a very obvious method, but it is surprising how many 'antique' lampshade covers on close inspection prove to be 'crackled' by this method.

Another method of crackling is the use of amyl acetate on spirit varnish. This method will produce closely patterned ridges and cracks. Spread a sheet of parchment on a smooth flat surface and apply a coat of clear cellulose or synthetic varnish, with a broad brush. Allow the varnish to thoroughly dry, then wipe amyl acetate on a piece of cloth, over the varnish. The amyl acetate reacts on the varnish base, and as it dries and evaporates, closely patterned ridges and cracks form, the fineness of the pattern depending on the amount of amyl acetate used. Usually the crackled pattern formed is very small, but if practice is carried out on odd pieces of parchment, using different kinds of synthetic varnishes, and varying the amount of amyl acetate used, the worker will find that it is possible to form an evenly patterned crackle effect over the surface of the material. It will be found in practice that in most cases the reaction of the amyl acetate on the varnish produces a series of ridges rather than cracks, but if care is taken, the ridges may be smoothed out by rubbing the material down with *very fine* glasspaper. After rubbing down, the cracks may be darkened by rubbing shoe polish into them. Apply the polish on a soft cloth and clean off the surplus before it hardens. Varnish to finish, but do not use synthetic varnish for the final coat.

A great deal of practice will be necessary, using odd scraps of parchment, before a high standard of efficiency in treating the material is attained, but the result of the method is far better than that of the first method. Frequent practice too, is necessary, before the next method is successfully used. It is perhaps the best method of all for the home craftworker, but —and I repeat—it will be necessary to become thoroughly acquainted with the method and the limitations of its application by frequent practice with odd pieces of parchment, before attempting the treatment of a shade cover.

It is necessary to work the third method in correct sequence, and it has been carefully set out below. Use good quality parchment paper which is fairly thick—if thin parchment paper is used, it may buckle. Make a weak solution of carpenter's glue and water, and before applying it, pin the corners of the parchment down to a firm flat surface. Use a clean wide brush, and apply the glue solution to the parchment—on one side only—while the liquid is still warm, but do not brush it on while *hot*. The glue solution should be only thinly applied. If too much is put on the parchment, it may cockle in drying. In drying, the glue coating should crack, forming irregular shapes. Cracking may also be done by pressing with the fingers on the back of the parchment, with the glue-covered side resting on a cloth. If this is done carefully, the crackle pattern will closely imitate that of antique parchment. If too much pressure is applied the crackle pattern will be fine and small. However, with practice on odd pieces of parchment, the craftworker will soon acquire the 'feel' of the process. When carrying out the crackle process to decorate a lampshade, it should be done on the cover, after it is fixed to the frame, but for the purpose of practice, the work may be carried out on odd scraps of parchment pinned to a table top. After the glue has cracked, the cracks should be treated to darken them. Black or brown shoe polish is suitable, but it should only be applied to a small area of the material at a time, and after filling the cracks, the surplus polish should be immediately removed. Different manufactures of carpenter's glues sometimes react in different ways, and according to the amount brushed on the surface of the material—also to the temperature of the room in which the work is carried out, and it may be necessary to apply gentle heat to the glued parchment. The decoration will be much more effective if the cracks are self-formed, as if the material has to be pressed with the fingers, the crackle pattern is often very small.

After darkening the cracks and allowing the polish to harden, the material should be given one or two coats of a good quality varnish, which serves to fix the crackled undercoat, and improve the appearance of the material. I repeat—**the secret of successfully crackling parchment is in practice.**

Painting on Parchment: Parchment paper is a very easy material on which to paint. The slightly oily mottled material forms an excellent background for painting with water colours, oil colours or spirit colours. When painting parchment paper, it should be remembered that the material is translucent, and if it is placed over a picture or pencilled design, the pattern will be clearly visible through the parchment. Sometimes, when decorating parchment, it is found difficult to apply the colours, which blob and become very unmanageable. This is due to the oil in the material, which forms a greasy film on the surface. Immediately before commencing to paint, and before the decoration pattern has been outlined on the material in pencil, the decoration area should be briskly rubbed with a soft rubber, and this will greatly assist in making the colours easy to manage.

When painting lampshades, it should be remembered that some colour values change in different lights; a colour may appear very suitable in natural light, but when the shade is in use over a lighted lamp, it may be found that the colour looks entirely different. Therefore, colours should be seen in natural and artificial light before using them to decorate a lampshade. Spirit colours are suitable for use on parchment, but they are very fast drying and the non-expert lampshade worker may prefer to use slower drying oil colours, or water colours. It should be remembered that some colours fade if exposed to strong light, and this is particularly true of glass painting colours; however, the fading is slight and large lampshades, where the cover is some distance from the lighted lamp bulb, may be decorated with these colours. Glass painting colours are transparent, and decorations painted with them are particularly attractive on parchment.

Decorative Thonging: The thonging materials used for securing lampshade covers to foundation frames may be worked in decorative patterns, and some suggestions for decorative thonging are illustrated in Fig. 31. By simply crossing the material, an attractive pattern is formed which may be improved upon by using thonging of two different colours. This is known as the crossed whip stitch in leatherwork, and other leatherwork stitches may be successfully used in lampshade making, such as double whip stitch, the running and whip stitch, buttonhole stitching, etc. These are quite attractive if worked with narrow plastic thonging or fine silk cords. Silk cords have many uses in lampshade making, and if ends are frayed to make tassels, the strands at the top of the tassels should be sealed with a little cellulose lacquer or nail varnish, to prevent them unravelling.

Other Materials: Many other materials may be used for decorating lampshades, and the ingenious craftworker will have no trouble in inventing ways for using all kinds of material. Here are some suggestions.

Lace may be used for decorating lampshades. It is obtainable in almost any colour and is particularly attractive when used over another material of a contrasting colour. Black lace over a cover of white buckram is very pleasing. It may be damped and pressed to the buckram or sandwiched between an outer cover of mat surface acetate and buckram.

Labels and postage stamps are suitable for decorating some kinds of lampshades. Foreign stamps or colourful hotel labels on a parchment cover, present novel forms of decoration. The lampshade should be given a coat of varnish after sticking the stamps or labels on the covering material, and the idea may be extended to include a 'calendar' cover by sticking the date sheets of a small calendar on the cover. Of course, such a lampshade would only be suitable for the year of the calendar currency, but lampshades of this nature would make excellent Christmas gifts.

Artificial flowers may be used for decorating some lampshades, providing they are well made and the colours are suitable, and I have seen some lampshades—large standards—with recesses cut in the cover in which rest artificial flowers protected by a 'window' of transparent acetate.

Silvery and golden stars, moons and signs of the zodiac make attractive additions to lampshades for use in bedrooms. Ideal materials for working these attractive decor motifs are **Winsor & Newton's "Saree Relief Colours"**. The **"Relief Colours"** may be applied direct from the tube or with a brush and provide an adhesive foundation upon which coloured lustre powders and metallic powders are scattered, and when the base has dried and hardened, the coloured powders are firmly embedded in the coloured foundation.

Shapes of one material may be very often affixed to a cover of another material in the form of appliqued decoration, and lampshades of this type are particularly suitable for use in nurseries and children's bedrooms.

There are many other ideas and suggestions to be found, by looking at all kinds of materials with a fresh eye, in considering their possibilities in making and decorating lampshades. Lampshade making is not a craft of limited scope and much depends on the individual craftworker in making the most of his materials. The craft is one which can bring unlimited pleasure in profitably occupying spare-time hours, no very great outlay is required in the first place, and because of the variety of the work, the lampshade maker should never be bored.

I hope you have enjoyed reading this book as much as I have enjoyed writing it, and if I can be of any assistance, please do not hesitate to write to me, c/o the Publishers, at the address given on the title page. If you experience any difficulties at all in obtaining any of the materials mentioned, I will be very pleased to put you in touch with the suppliers.

LAMPSHADE MAKING

BOOK NUMBER TWO

BY

F. J. CHRISTOPHER, F.R.S.A.

Editor of *Popular Handicrafts* Magazine

CONTENTS

	PAGE
Preface	vii
Chapter I	9

Purpose and function of lampshades — points to consider — variety and scope — shades for particular purposes — materials — profitable lampshade making — care in working.

Chapter II 11

Making lampshade frames: Types of frames — welded frames — soldered frames — solderless frames — tools and equipment — materials — lampshade frame wire — description and sizes — parts of frames — fittings and attachments — making a soldered frame — parts and sizes — types of joints — shaping the wires — supporting the wires — use of "jigs" — assembly — panelled lampshade — shaped parts — jointing device. Frames without solder — suitable types — wire thicknesses — square-pendant shade — shaping the parts — assembly.

Chapter III 25

Covering materials: Choice and individual requirements — types of material — plastics — "Crinothene" — heat sealing — "Rilfoil" — description and uses — Cellulose Acetate and its use in lampshade making. Fabrics for lampshade making — parchment, vellum and papers — other materials. Braid, gimp and trimmings.

Chapter IV 30

Making patterns: Importance of accuracy — variation of sizes of sides and panels — treatment of differing materials — main types of foundation frames — popular shapes — patterns for "Empire" covers — curved panel patterns — patterns for fluted lampshade covers — formula for any-size fluted covers.

Chapter V 37

Simple lampshades: A thonged pendant shade — checking the frame — binding — pattern making — marking and cutting the material — punching the thong holes — thonging — sequence of work — use of plastic thonging. Covering an "Empire" frame — material — inspection — binding the frame — making the pattern — attaching the cover.

v

CONTENTS

PAGE

Chapter VI **44**
Lampshades with stitched covers: Bed-lamp shade — preparation — choice of material — making patterns — stitching — decoration. Another bed-lamp shade — inspecting the frame — binding — sewing — attaching net frill. Standard-lamp shade — curved and rounded panels — checking the frame — binding — thonging and stitching — decoration.

Chapter VII **52**
Fabric-covered lampshades: Materials — binding the frame — making the pattern — covering the frame — trimming. A bowl-shaped shade. Another method of making fabric-covered lampshades. Novelty methods — using lace or net over stiff paper.

Chapter VIII **64**
Stiff lampshade covers: Paper shades — pleated lampshade — pie-frill lampshade covers — "Coolie Hat" type of cover — fluted shade in buckram — velvet and parchment shade.

Chapter IX **72**
Basketry lampshades: Lampshade for a reading lamp — materials — method of weaving the shade — constructing the base — finishing — wiring and lampholder.

Chapter X **76**
Table lamp bases: Converting bottles and jars — fitting a lamp socket and switch — "Pifco" adaptor — use of a back-plate — drilling a hole for the flex — suitable drills — precautions.

Chapter XI **80**
Decorating lampshades: Tinting — painted designs — transfers — coloured paper shades — floral motifs — repeating design — wax crayon designs — fringes and braids — lace decoration — "shadow" work — gathered or pleated frills — ruching — shell edging — Toby frills — knitted fringe.

PREFACE

ONE of the most interesting handicrafts of recent years is that of making lampshades. Although lampshades have been made as long as lamps have existed, it was not until the immediate postwar period that the craft reached such a high degree of popularity. It has now almost assumed the proportions of a small industry.

Thousands of people are now making lampshades at home for a variety of reasons, which embrace the high cost of shop-bought shades, the urge to do some useful form of handiwork, and the need to supplement slender incomes. Whatever the reason for the present great increase of interest in lampshade making, there is no doubt that it is one of the pleasantest of all home occupations. The materials are not costly, the work is clean, quiet and light, and the finished products amply recompense the worker for the cost of materials and the time expended.

I should like to make it quite clear that *Lampshade Making Book Number Two* is quite complete in itself, and that it does not have to be read and used as a textbook together with my first book *Lampshade Making*, also published by Foyles, although I am quite sure that the beginner and the expert will find much of constructional interest in both books.

F. J. C.

BOURNEMOUTH, 1953.

CHAPTER I

Purpose and function of lampshades — points to consider — variety and scope — shades for particular purposes — materials — profitable lampshade making — care in working.

IN the first place, it is essential to appreciate the function of the products before commencing to make lampshades. It would obviously be as foolish to perch a small candle-shade on a tall and stately standard as it would be to reverse the process, yet many lampshade makers—professional and amateur—do just as foolish things in making their wares.

Not nearly enough time and thought are given to the purpose of the shade before embarking on the actual making of it. Frames are covered, often very well, but without any very clear idea as to where and how that particular shade is to be used. There are exceptions, of course, but for the most part those who do genuinely plan and visualize a shade as part of a whole lampstand, which is in turn part of a furnished room, are the exceptions rather than the rule. Yet when the making of lampshades is being taken up either as a hobby or as a means of combining pleasure with a profitable spare-time business, it is impossible to overstress the importance of looking upon lampshades as important pieces of furnishings in a home, rather than looking upon them as oddments thrown in when the main furnishing has been completed. If you have in your mind's eye a view of the complete room in which it is intended to put the lampshade, you will make just the shade which will fit and finish that furnishing scheme.

If you are making your lampshades for re-sale, it is an excellent plan to collect as many coloured pictures of rooms from magazines as you can find. Then, before commencing a shade, select a picture of a room, and make your shade to fit that room. In recent years great improvements have been made in lighting, and now nearly every home has a wide variety of lights for which lampshades will be required.

The shading of lights is a matter depending a great deal on personal tastes, but a few general rules can be observed with advantage. First, avoid materials which will give a cold, harsh light, and choose instead those that, while in no way impairing the light, cause a soft diffusion of light. For example, a light glowing softly through parchment or amber "Crinothene" in an entrance hall is a much more pleasing and welcoming sight than a plain white lamp would be.

Shades for dining rooms should be not too dressed up and fussy, but at the same time pleasantly warm-looking. Any of the creamy-coloured parchments, ivory "Crinothene" and pinky peach-coloured materials will look well, no matter whether made in paper, plastics or fabrics.

For use in sitting rooms, where reading, needlework and other activities have to be catered for, it is essential that the lampshade should shade the lamps but not obscure the light. Lampshades for the bedroom can be, and usually are, more decorative. They can be as fancy as you wish. Nowadays there is a wide variety of lamps used in a bedroom—bedside lamps, bedhead lamps, lamps to stand on dressing tables and, of course, the ordinary pendant lamps.

Well designed and made lampshades can add considerable charm to a home, and there is certainly a great satisfaction in being able to turn out a beautiful luxury-type lampshade at an economical price. There are many lovely fabrics to choose from, and a very wide range of plastics and parchment-type papers, while lampshades of basket work, raffia and string are all becoming very popular.

Apart from the great sense of satisfaction obtained by making something beautiful and of practical utility, the lampshade maker will find that there is the basis of a very profitable spare-time business in this craft. The work itself is absorbing, and the materials and equipment on the whole inexpensive. Lampshade making is clean and light to do, and can be carried out at odd intervals, without the necessity of setting up an elaborate workroom. One other advantage is that you can start off on the making of a lampshade right away; there is no great amount of tedious practising to this craft. But care in cutting out materials and neatness in working are the only ways in which you can turn out a perfect lampshade.

CHAPTER II

Making lampshade frames: Types of frames — welded frames — soldered frames — solderless frames — tools and equipment — materials — lampshade frame wire — description and sizes — parts of frames — fittings and attachments — making a soldered frame — parts and sizes — types of joints — shaping the wires — supporting the wires — use of "jigs" — assembly — panelled lampshade — shaped parts — jointing device. Frames without solder — suitable types — wire thicknesses — square-pendant shade — shaping the parts — assembly.

THE instructions given in this chapter are for making lampshade foundation frames. It should first be fully appreciated that complete lampshade frames of all kinds, shapes and sizes for every purpose are quite easily obtainable locally, and from mail-order suppliers who specialize in the sale of handicraft lampshade materials. This chapter, then, is included for those workers who would rather make their own frames, or who wish to make a foundation frame for a lampshade of particular design for a special purpose.

The making of lampshade frames is not too difficult a task for the average home worker to tackle, and a certain amount of equipment, and the use of some tools—other than those used in covering lampshades—is required. The kind of equipment and tools will vary to some extent with the type of frame-making adopted. Frame-making can roughly be divided into three main groups, according to the nature of the jointing of the wires. These groups are:

  A. Frames with welded joints.
  B. Frames with soldered joints.
  C. Other types of joint.

Of these, the first method of making frames with welded joints is usually beyond the scope of the average home-worker. Welded frames are jointed by a process known as "Spot-Welding" (a method of jointing metals by melting and "fusing" the ends of the wire), which requires the use of semi-industrial equipment. This is not described here, as information about the setting up of plant and equipment for spot-welding can be obtained from the manufacturers of such equipment.

Methods B and C are those most suitable for the worker at

home, and these may be simplified in description by describing them as *making frames with solder* and *making frames without solder*. For both kinds of frame-making a pair of really good pliers, such as those illustrated in Fig. 1 (with strong jaws and side cutting edges), will be required. These are used for cutting and bending wires. A smaller pair of pliers may also be required, but these are not essential to commence with.

For soldered frames it will be necessary to use a soldering iron, and an electrically heated iron, such as the type illustrated in Fig. 1, is best if many frames are to be made. When buying an

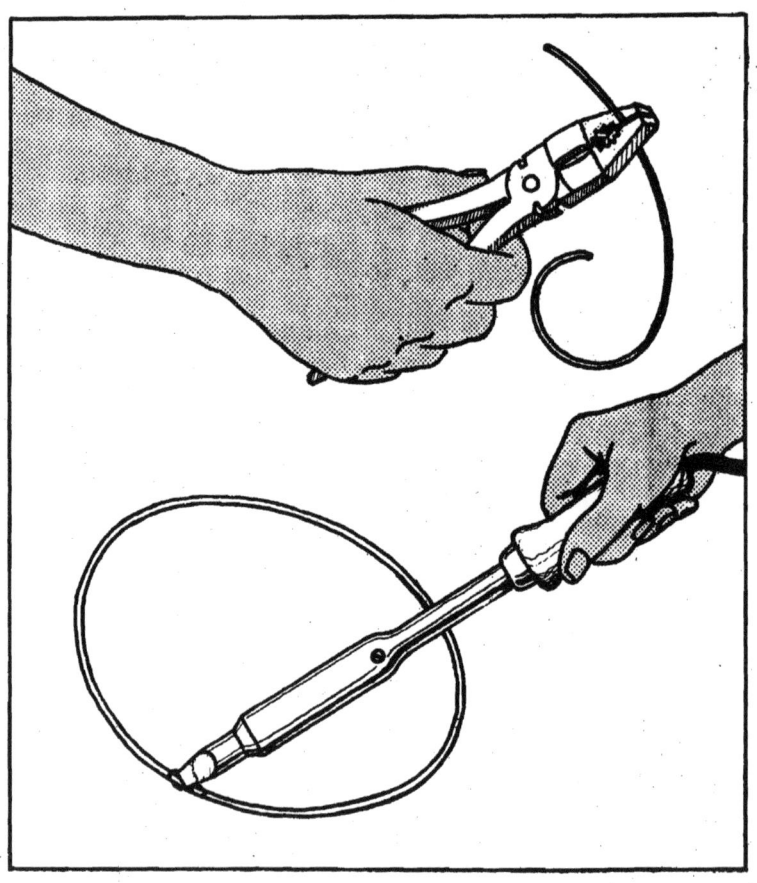

FIG. 1. TOOLS IN USE

electric soldering iron, make certain that it is suitable for use with the voltage of the house mains. A 60-watt soldering iron will provide a steady heat to the "bit." The soldering iron should be properly connected to a three-point plug to ensure that it is safely earthed before use.

Solder and flux are required for making soldered frames. These materials may be purchased together in the form of "cored" solder, which is supplied as coils of tube solder, the centre of the tube being filled with flux. The use of solder of this kind enables the worker to make good strong joints in less time than in using solder and flux separately.

The main essential in making lampshade frames is, of course, wire. Not any old wire will do. The most suitable wire is mild-steel tinned wire which can be easily bent to shape and will readily "take" soldering. This wire is usually obtainable locally in coils varying in weight from 1 to 28 lb. When buying wire, make sure it has a bright, shiny surface, or it may be difficult to work and solder. Copper wire is also suitable for lampshade making. All kinds of wire should be stored flat and should be kept away from anything of a corrosive or greasy nature.

The wire used for making a lampshade foundation frame must obviously be suitable in thickness and strength for the particular size and type of lampshade being made. To give a simple example, it would be foolish to use wire light enough for a candle lampshade for a large frame for a standard lamp. The following is a guide to suitability of wire gauges for frames for particular purposes (the abbreviation s.w.g. stands for Standard Wire Gauge).

For large frames, suitable for standard-lamp shades, large pendant-lamp shades and large table-lamp shades—in fact, for all large shades—12 s.w.g. should be used.

For frames of medium size, such as those for shades for pendant- and table-lamp use, and for some kinds of bed lamps, 14 s.w.g. should be used.

For making small frames for use on wall lamps, small candle lamps on chandeliers, and most kinds of bed lamps, wire of 16 s.w.g. should be used.

These wire gauges only apply to wire used for making soldered frames. Frames without solder require the use of thinner wire, and this will be fully described later in this chapter.

There are, of course, many kinds of frames for different purposes, and these are shown in some of the illustrations throughout

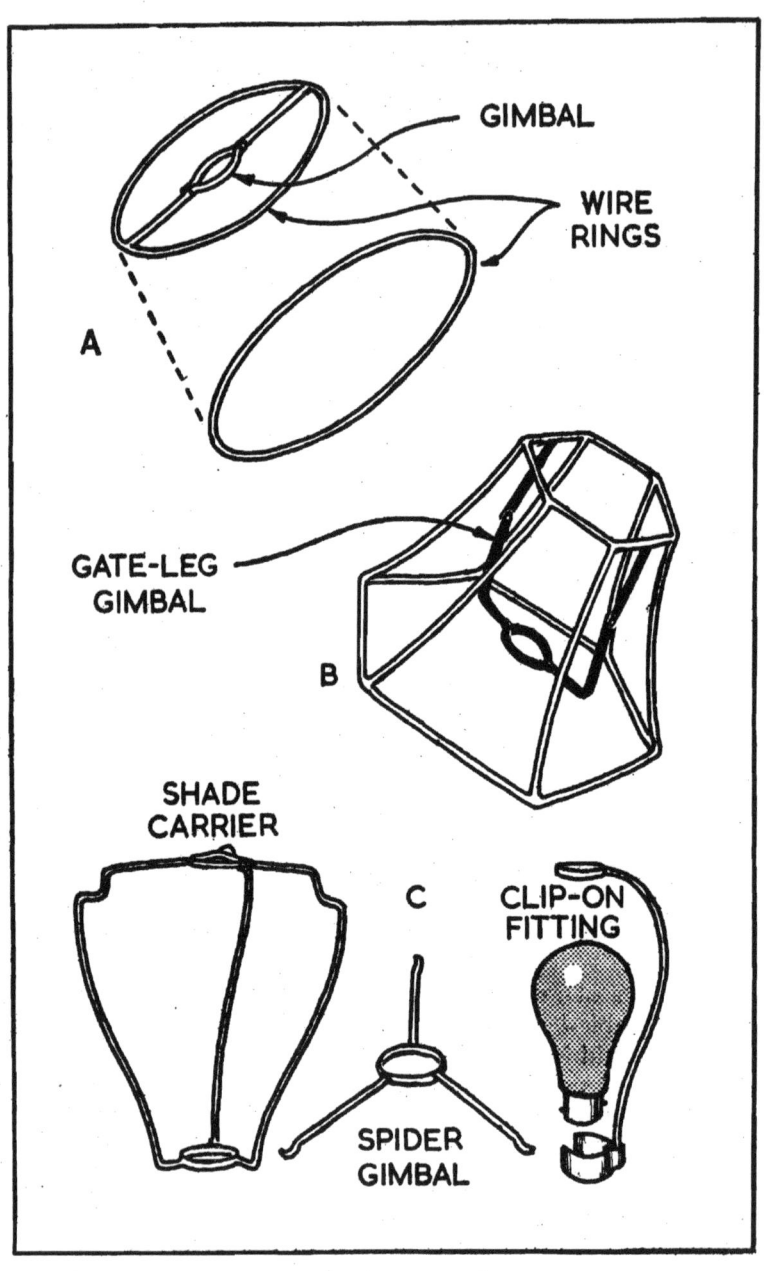

FIG. 2. FRAMES AND FITTINGS

this book. Fig. 2 shows some typical frames and illustrates the main features general to all types of frames. Fig. 2a shows an exploded "Empire" frame which has a "top member" in the shape of a ring, a "base member" also circular in shape, and a "gimbal." The gimbal is simply a small wire ring which is attached to the top member by a short piece of wire either side of the top. The gimbal fits over the lamp-holder socket and is held in place on the socket with a screwed retaining ring.

Fig. 2b shows a frame with shaped "side members" which divide the frame into panels. This frame has no top gimbal ring fitted to the top member, but it is shown fitted with a "gate-leg" gimbal. This form of gimbal fitting, which is hinged, allows the frame to be used for a table lamp. Gate-leg gimbals can be purchased ready-made for attachment by soldering to frames made at home.

Fig. 2c shows other types of fittings for use with lampshade frames of different types, including a "spider gimbal," which allows the top member of a frame to rest in grooves at the ends of the arms, a "clip-on" fitment for very small shades, a "shade carrier" for use with large standard lamps. The gimbal attachment can be fitted to a pendant lamp to convert it to use over a table lamp. These are the main fitments. Any others are mentioned in later chapters describing their uses.

To make a soldered lampshade it is necessary to cut wires to length for the various parts of the frame, bend the wires to shape, and solder each joint. Therefore, when cutting wires to length, it will be necessary to allow extra for any overlapping joints. To illustrate the making of a lampshade frame, the construction of an "Empire" shade with side members is described and the parts are illustrated in Fig. 3.

This lampshade has a top diameter of 5 in., the base has a diameter of 8 in., and the sides of the lampshade are also 8 in. Nine pieces of wire are required to make the frame. These pieces are: one for the top, one for the base, four pieces (one for each) for the side members, a piece for the gimbal, and two short pieces for the gimbal supports. The piece of wire for the top should measure 5 in. by $3\frac{1}{7}$ in. plus $\frac{1}{4}$ in., which allows for overlapping the joint. Therefore this piece should be just over 16 in. long. The piece for the circular base should be 8 in. by $3\frac{1}{7}$ in. plus $\frac{1}{4}$ in. (about $25\frac{1}{4}$ in.), which is equal to the circumference plus $\frac{1}{4}$ in. for overlapping. The pieces for the side members should be 8 in. long plus

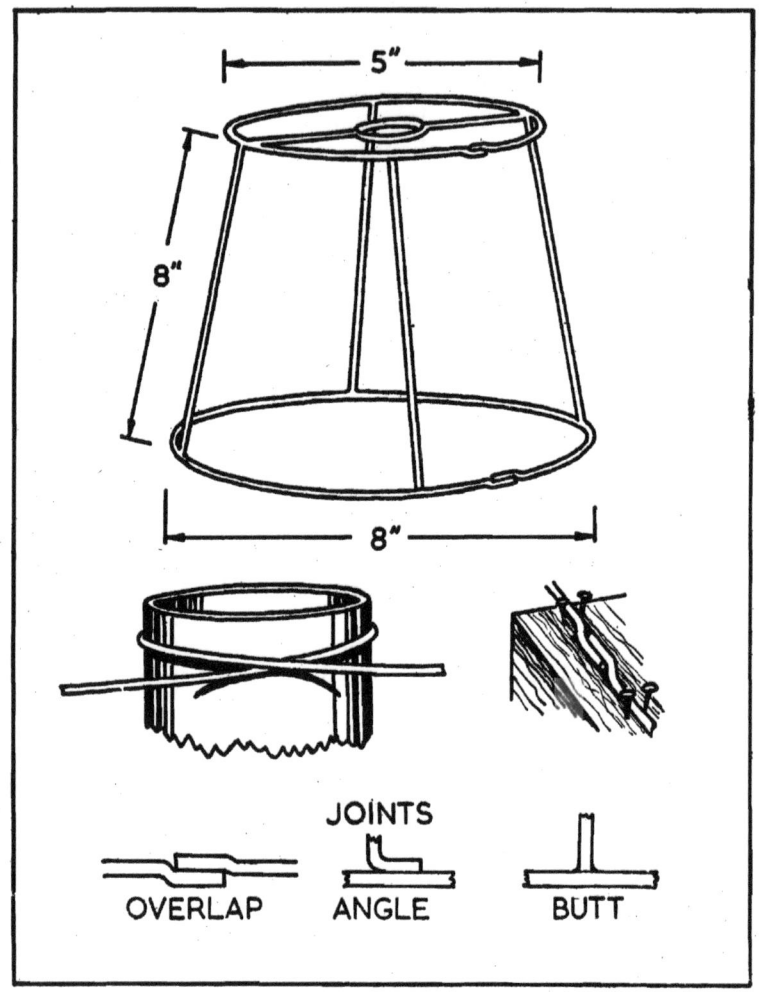

FIG. 3. EXPLODED "EMPIRE"

¾ in., which allows ⅜ in. at each end of the wire to bend over for jointing. The diameter of the small gimbal ring should be 1⅛ in., and the supporting pieces which hold the gimbal in place on the top ring should be 2 in. to allow for overlapping joints.

The illustration Fig. 3 shows how all the joints of the lampshade are made. The top ring and the base ring both have overlapping joints, and the wire should be bent to the shape shown in the illustration. The side members can be bent over at right angles at top and bottom to make the joints shown, or they could simply be "butted" on to the wire. The gimbal-ring supporting pieces are attached under the top ring and under the gimbal ring.

To make the frame it will be necessary to shape the top and base, and this can be done by bending the wires round a tin of suitable size (smaller than the size of the finished piece), as shown in the illustration. If this is done successfully, perfect circles should be formed. The next part of the work consists of soldering the joints of the top and base rings, and the appearance of the finished joint where the wires overlap is shown in the illustration.

To hold the wires in place while the ends are being soldered, four nails should be hammered into a piece of wood or bench top as shown. With the ends of the top and base rims firmly and neatly soldered, the side members should be attached. To do this accurately it will be necessary to support the wires by means of wooden shapes. These shapes are shown in Fig. 4, where it will be seen that for the frame described it will be necessary to cut two pieces of wood to shape and fit them together with a simple halved joint. This will suffice to hold the top and bottom rings in position, and the ends of the shaped pieces of wood will form a rest for the side members, which may then be soldered to the main frame. The last piece to make is the gimbal, and the small ring may be shaped by bending the wire over a piece of round wood such as a broom handle. With this done, the ends of the gimbal ring should be soldered and the two supporting wires attached first to the ring, then to the top of the frame.

Once the wooden pattern or "jig" has been made it can be used for making hundreds of lampshades of the same size and shape. For each different shape or size made it will be necessary to construct another simple wood pattern so that the parts may be held in place while the joints are being soldered.

Also shown in Fig. 4 is a wooden jig for a shaped frame, and these two illustrations should be sufficient to give the frame maker the idea of the process of construction. In the case of "Empire" frames without side-members, special jigs can be made for the top and bottom rings. These consist of a circular piece of wood lipped with a piece of three-ply, and if necessary the top of the centre piece can be protected by adding asbestos.

It is quite a simple matter to shape a piece of wire for the round "Empire" frame, but it will be found rather more difficult to

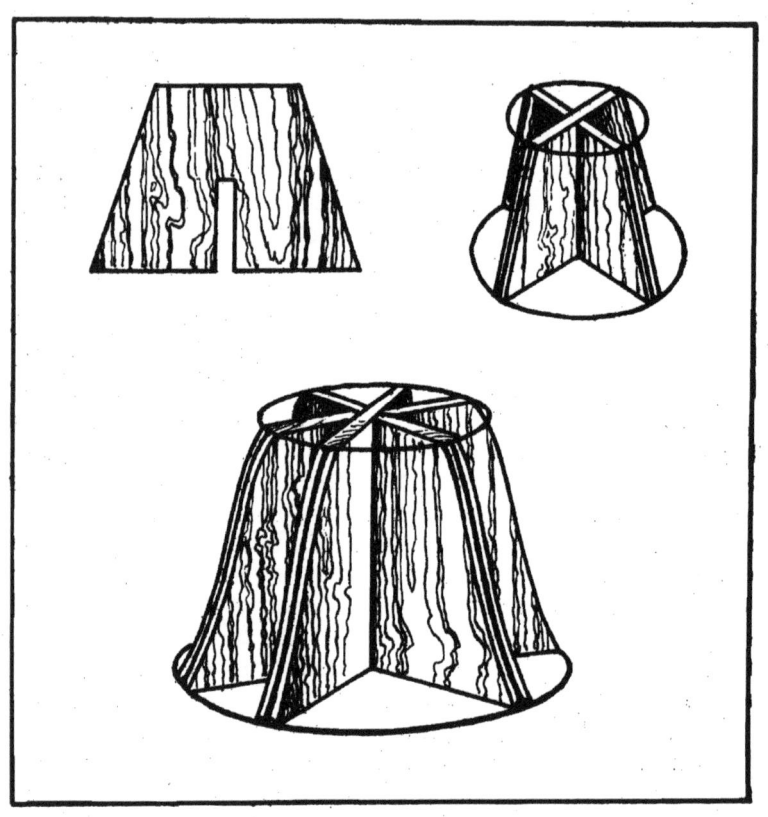

FIG. 4. WOOD SHAPES

shape wires for other types of frame, such as the panel frame illustrated in Fig. 5, which has a shaped top and base and side members. To shape the scalloped base it will be necessary to cut a piece of wood to the shape of a semicircle and attach it to a bench top. With this done, two nails or screws should be firmly positioned as shown in the illustration (Fig. 5). The wire for the base is then cut to length and shaped by inserting one end between one of the nails and the jig, bending it firmly round the part of the wood shape, then bending the end of the wire down to form the end of the scallop. This is repeated to form all the scallops of the frame to shape.

For the side members it will be necessary to make a two-part

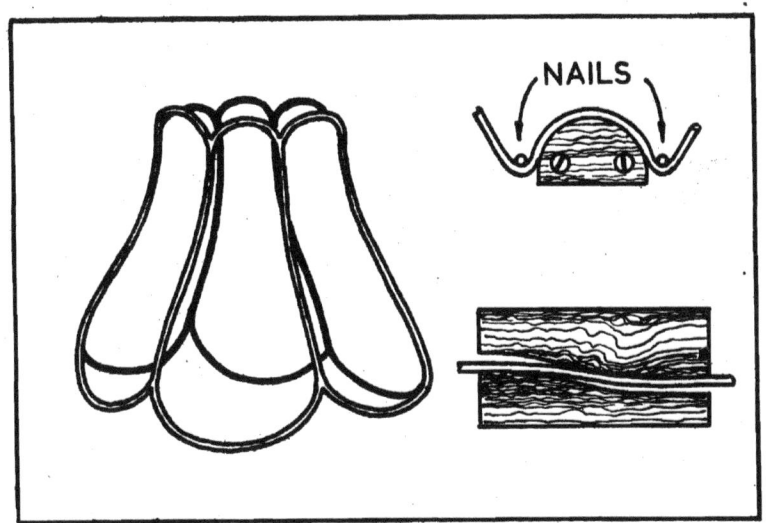

FIG. 5. PANELLED FRAME

jig. This is illustrated in Fig. 5. It consists simply of two pieces of wood which are cut to the shape of the side member so that they fit together snugly. With these made, the wire is then cut to length, placed between the two pieces of the jig, which are then placed in a bench vice and forced together. Obviously, a very hard wood should be used for making parts of the jig, or alternatively the shaped sides may be protected with a strip of thin metal. Of course, it will be necessary to make a set of jigs and patterns for each frame being made, if it is intended to practise this part of the craft as a commercial venture. If only one or two frames of the same shape and size are being made, it is not necessary to go to all the trouble of making jigs. It should be possible for the worker to shape the parts by hand with a pair of pliers, and in the case of shaped side members and bases, pattern outlines can be drawn on a stiff piece of paper and wire bent to these shapes.

All the parts of panelled lampshades should be firmly soldered together.

Another method of jointing wires in lampshade making, if only a few are being made, can be done by using a simple device known as the "Wirejoint," and this is illustrated in Fig. 6. By this method, thin lampshade wires can be joined together in a matter of seconds

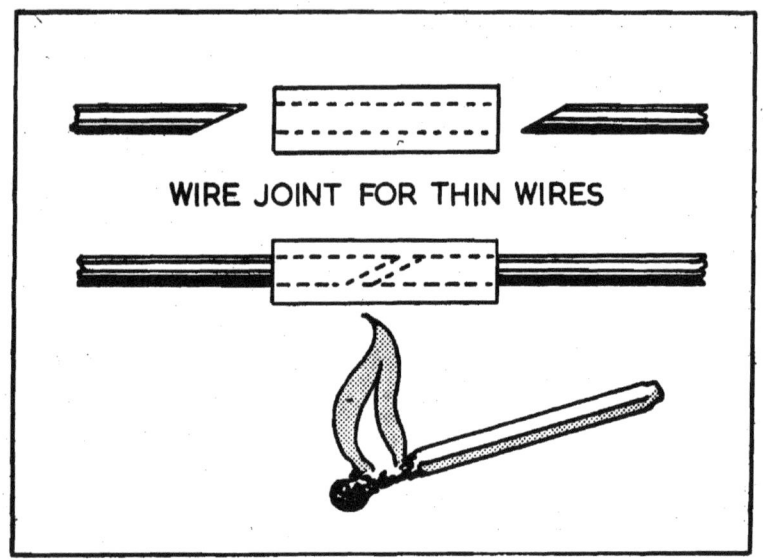

FIG. 6. WIRE JOINT

with a perfect soldered joint in one operation, using no other tools than a lighted match. The "Wirejoint" consists of a ceramic insulating tube or connector, which contains a central lining of solder and non-corrosive flux. The ends of the wires should overlap inside the tube. The use of a match completes the joint.

Although to make any quantity of wire lampshade frames requires a soldering iron, the home craftsman who wishes to make just a few frames can quite easily do this by the solderless method here described. This is not suitable for all types of frames, but quite a variety of bed lamps, table lamps and pendant shades can be made by this method.

Fig. 7 shows several suitable styles, and although the instructions given here are for a square pendant, the other types are just as easy to make. For making these frames without solder, you will need a pair of side-cutting pliers, a ruler, a pair of scissors, some insulating tape, some bias tape and, of course, the necessary wire. When purchasing the wire it should be ensured that it is the correct gauge for the type of frame you wish to make. Generally speaking, all small frames, such as those for candle lamps, wall lamps and the small types of bed lamps which are soldered, are made from 16 s.w.g. wire, but for making these without solder, 18 s.w.g. is recommended. Medium-sized frames, such as the larger-type bed lamps, table lamps, pendant lamps and some styles of hanging bowl shades which are soldered, are best made with 14 s.w.g., but for solderless frames you are advised to use 16 s.w.g. However, should you decide on a large frame, either a hanging bowl shape or a standard lampshade which, when soldered, is normally made from 12 s.w.g. wire, for a solderless frame you should use 14 s.w.g. It is important that the correct thickness of wire is used in each case. These are, however, only intended as a guide, and if you are making an in-between-sized frame you must select the most suitable thickness of wire for the particular type and purpose of the shade. Generally speaking, for

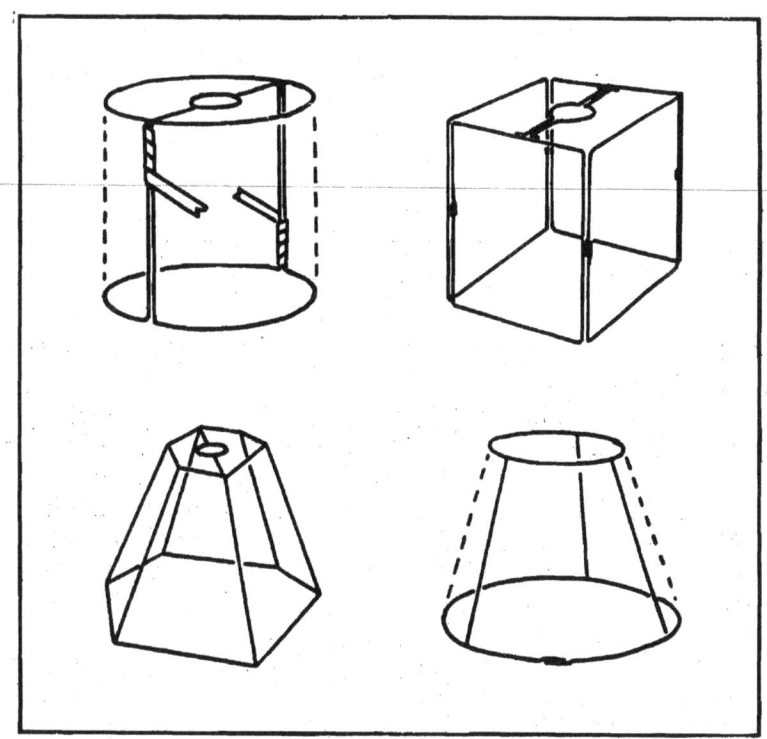

FIG. 7. SOLDERLESS FRAMES

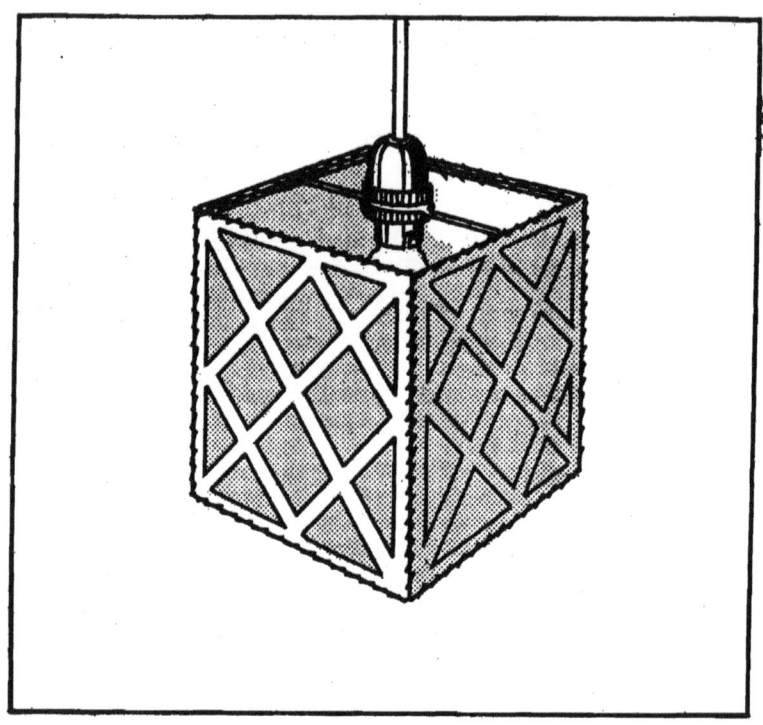

FIG. 8. FRAME WITHOUT SOLDER

solderless frames a thinner wire is used than that used for a soldered frame.

The frame shown in Fig. 8 is a very simple square pendant type. This type of frame is very suitable for use in an entrance hall, and frames of this type may be covered with a great variety of materials. It is a very useful basic shape, and can be made in any size. The frame is made by forming the wire to the shape of each part separately and then binding them together. Exact dimensions are not given, as the lampshade maker will probably wish to make a frame to fit personal requirements.

Commence by making six squares of wire, one for each side (these obviously must match exactly) and the top and base. The corners are bent with the pliers, and it may be necessary to make several adjustments to ensure accurate fitting when assembling. It is best to make the gimbal after the frame has been assembled. This assures accurate fitting. Now take all the parts and try them against each other to ensure that they will make an accurate whole. The frame is assembled by binding the parts together with adhesive tape.

To assemble, take two squares and bind them together top and bottom with insulating tape, as shown in the illustration Fig. 9. Bind the adhesive tape tightly at the corners and ends of the wires. It is never necessary to bind all the wire, but you must to some extent use your own judgment as to the exact amount of binding required for any one frame. Overlap the tape when binding, as this avoids a lumpy joint, which may show when the shade is covered. Join the other squares to the frame in the same manner. It will be necessary to bind them very carefully to avoid getting the joints large and lumpy. Fig. 9 shows the steps in binding

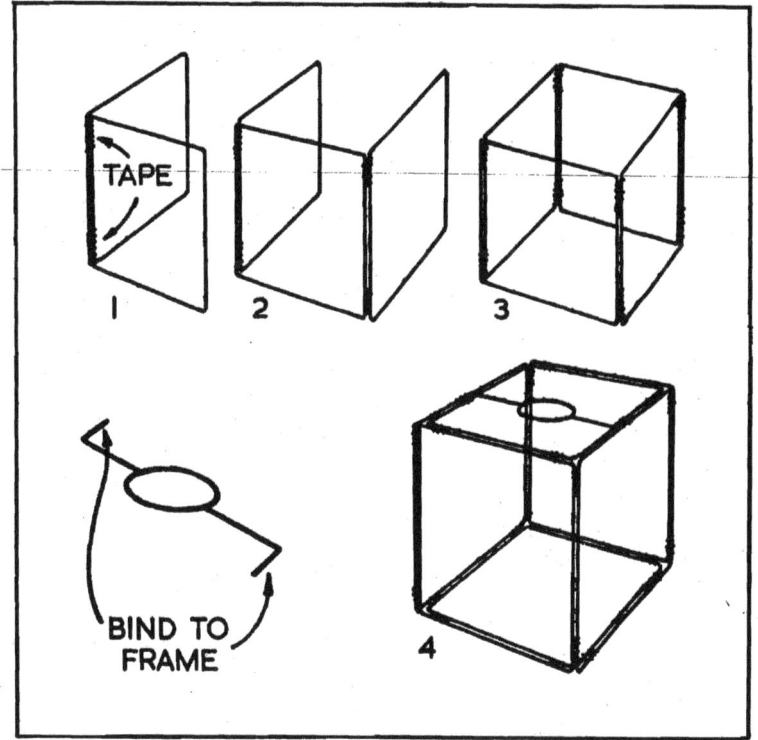

FIG. 9. JOINING THE PARTS

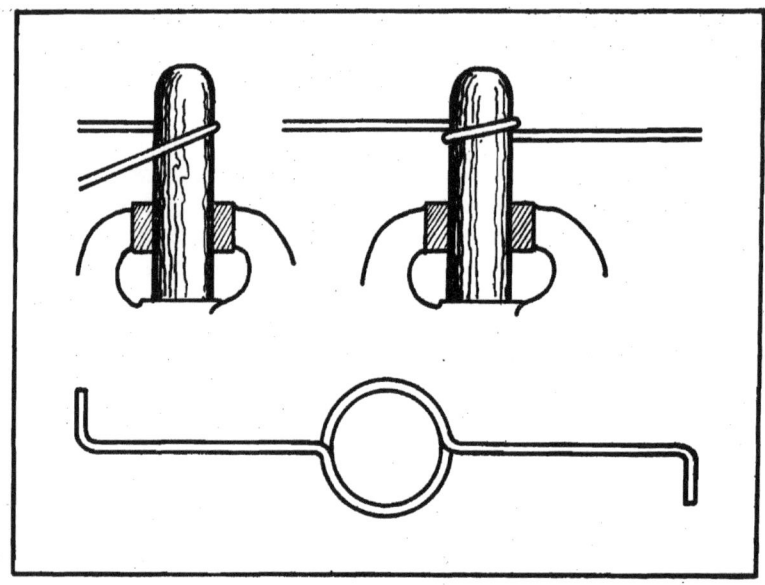

FIG. 10. ONE PIECE GIMBAL

the parts together. Place the gimbal ring in position and bind carefully. The frame is now complete and ready for binding with bias tape before covering, and all the wires should be bound except the gimbal ring, to make the frame firm and rigid.

The gimbal ring and supports can be made in one piece and the ends bent over for attachment to the frame. A method of making one-piece gimbals for this type of frame and others is illustrated in Fig. 10. To make this type of gimbal a piece of round wood should be secured to a flat piece of wood. The round piece should be $1\frac{1}{4}$ in. in diameter. The wire—of suitable gauge for the type of frame being made—should be placed against the front of the round piece of wood and the ends bent to form an inverted U. The ends should then be crossed at the front of the shaping piece, then each wire bent with pliers at right angles to the ring.

CHAPTER III

Covering materials: Choice and individual requirements — types of material — plastics — "Crinothene" — heat sealing — "Rilfoil" — description and uses — Cellulose Acetate and its use in lampshade making. Fabrics for lampshade making — parchment, vellum and papers — other materials. Braid, gimp and trimmings.

THE covering of lampshades for the home is very much a matter of personal taste and suitability. It is difficult to make hard-and-fast rules as to which materials are best for lampshade covering. Some are perhaps more practical in use than others, but even the value of durability is debatable. After all, it may be that one prefers a shade which is pretty but will last only a short time and then have to be re-covered, rather than to have a plainer shade which will last for years.

Lampshades have been made from practically every material—string, raffia, cane, "Cellophane," wood, and many others. Roughly speaking, they fall into four groups—plastics, fabrics, papers and miscellaneous.

Plastics are perhaps the most popular at present, and there is a huge variety offered by the manufacturers. "Crinothene" is probably the best-known plastic covering, and it certainly has much to recommend it, because of the ease with which even the most inexperienced person can work it and its wide colour range of soft pastel shades which do not colour the light given out by the lamp. "Crinothene" has very great light-diffusion properties and is in every way suitable for covering lampshades.

"Crinothene" is a flexible sheet material; it is very tough, though having a very dainty appearance; it is non-tacky, durable and light. The surface has an attractive patterned, crêpe-like appearance, and is produced in many lovely shades—blue, pink, peach, amber, green, mauve, ivory and natural. It is easily washed in warm soapy water without fear of damage, distortion or fading. "Crinothene" does not contain any plasticizer, and under normal conditions will show no signs of hardening with age or becoming brittle. It is sold by all handicraft dealers by the yard. The width is normally 34 in., while the thickness of the material averages about 0 030 in. "Crinothene" may be cut easily with scissors or knife and can be punched and stapled without any difficulty. A wax pencil or chalk are the most suitable for tracing patterns on to the material.

"Crinothene" can be stitched with cotton or wire, the most satisfactory joint being obtained by six to eight stitches to the inch. Satisfactory joints can also be made by heat-sealing in the following manner. Fasten your material so that the overlapping edges are held firmly in place. The heat-sealing may be done with a heated tool; an ordinary soldering iron, the type which is heated over a gas ring, may be used, or if you work carefully a clean poker will do the job. However, to obtain the best results an electrically heated soldering iron should be used. Whichever tool you use, obviously it must be clean, and it will be necessary to experiment on a spare piece of "Crinothene."

After heating the tool, turn off the heat and commence working the material. Start at the top of the joint and work down, using a stroking movement with the tool. Do not press the tool into the material. Now work along the joint on the inside. Next, on the right side of the "Crinothene," and using a heated small modelling tool or steel knitting needle, roughen the surface of the joint. Leave the "Crinothene" to cool and harden. The strength of the bond obtained by heat-sealing is the same as that of the "Crinothene" itself.

There is no really satisfactory adhesive for "Crinothene," although it is possible to use pressure-sensitive adhesives such as "Mystic" for sticking on labels, braids and fringes.

"Rilfoil" is another plastic product very suitable for lampshade making. It is a semi-rigid material and is embossed in two patterns, linen and parchment. It is sold by the yard, at a width of 36 in. The wide range of colours includes white, cream, amber, orange, peach, green, pink and blue. This plastic material is not highly inflammable and is easily cut and shaped to any style of frame. Like "Crinothene," it is very easy to keep clean with warm water and soap flakes, and is very long lasting.

Yet another plastic material suitable for covering lampshades is Acetate. Cellulose Acetate in sheet form is very popular with lampshade makers. This is a plastic material which is manufactured with an almost endless variety of surfaces and colours. Replicas of lace, chintz, leather, etc., are all obtainable in Acetate. This material is not highly inflammable, is very strong, but has one drawback—it cracks very easily if creased. It can be decorated by painting or with transfers. It is best joined by thonging with plastic thongs. Acetate may be cut with a sharp knife or with scissors, or if the surface is scratched with a sharp-pointed tool and the material bent away from the scratch, it will break along the scratch line.

Fabric-covered shades are perhaps the most elaborate and beautiful. A great variety of fabrics is suitable for this purpose. All kinds of silks are very popular, while ginghams, chintz, buckram, crêpes, muslin and lace can all be used with great success in the making of lampshades. They may be used separately or together. Almost any fabric that will permit the passage of light is suitable for covering shades. If it is very thin the shade may be lined with a fine material such as lawn or muslin. When lace or silk net are used they are usually placed over a buckram base, as the materials are not strong enough on their own.

Parchment vellum and stiff art papers are all used extensively for covering lampshades. Amongst this group are to be found old maps, manuscripts and deeds. Real parchments are skins, usually from goats, which have been specially treated so that they are soft, smooth and supple. These are expensive and not easy to come by. The finest qualities are called vellum. However, most arts and crafts stockists list parchment and vellum, and although these are really a form of treated paper, they are excellent for lampshade making, and can be purchased in a variety of colours and mottled patterns. Parchment paper is sold in sheets of various sizes, generally about 50 in. by 20 in., and is obtainable in several qualities. It is not advisable to use the cheapest kinds for lampshade covering, as these crack and discolour very quickly. The price is very economical, and it is one of the most popular lampshade covering materials, lending itself very readily to many methods of decoration. It can be painted with oil colours and spirit colours, or transfers can be used. Parchments and vellums may be enriched by tinting the insides of the shades. This is best done in pink or pale yellow. Designs are easily traced on parchment papers, as the material is translucent, and if the design is placed under the material it can be seen through, and the outlines of the design can then be pencilled in very lightly.

Parchment is obtainable in a wide assortment of colours and also embossed with various surface designs. It can be cut with a sharp knife, a razor blade or scissors.

Thick, good-quality cartridge paper and artists' paper are becoming very popular for making the Scandinavian type of pleated lampshades that have become so fashionable. They can be made translucent by soaking in oil and varnishing, but are mostly used in the natural state.

There are fashions in lampshades as in anything else, and it is now not unusual to see lampshades made from raffia, string, cane, wood veneer, knitted yarns and crochet cottons, and many other materials not usually associated with lampshade covers. The range of materials suitable for covering lampshades is limited only by the individual worker's resourcefulness. Cellophane is often used for shades, when a fancy, not too permanent, covering is required. The Cellophane, which is obtainable in many colours or clear, is used over a cover of stiff paper. A very attractive effect is obtained by using a contrasting coloured paper. The seam of the paper cover is gummed and the cover stitched to the frame. The Cellophane is then pleated or gathered round the shade and held in place by transparent adhesive tape. The shades are completed by adding velvet ribbon over the tape or by making a plait of five strips of Cellophane and sewing these plaits round top and bottom of the shade.

When planning lampshades, colour is very important. The colour of the covering material must tone with the trimmings and also with the general colour scheme of the room in which it is to be used, and it is always advisable to inspect all coloured materials in both day and artificial light. Some coloured materials may look completely different in changes of light.

Most lampshades are joined to the frame by stitching or thonging, and most sewing cottons are suitable for this. Dyed leather thonging can be used but is rather expensive; however, there are many coloured plastic thongings which are sold by the yard and which are very inexpensive, washable and easy to work.

Braids, cords, fringes and fancy trimmings for lampshades are in good supply and in an infinite variety of colours, patterns and widths. Fringes are purely decorative and can be used singly or double—*e.g.*, a fringe of $1\frac{1}{2}$ in. covered by a contrasting coloured fringe of 1 in. But braids, cords and gimps serve a dual purpose, giving decoration and at the same time providing a way of neatening joints and edges, by covering them.

When string and raffia are used to make shades, the wire frame is first painted a suitable colour, then the raffia or string is wound round and round until the frame is covered. Both these materials can be crocheted or knitted to make covers. Old maps and deeds make some lovely shades, used either alone or with velvet or velour.

Various silk nets can be made into beautiful shades by darning in the forms of a pattern, in coloured silks.

Whatever material is chosen for the cover, the lampshade maker will be well on the way to producing perfect shades if the preparatory work of selecting frames, materials and trimmings is given careful thought.

CHAPTER IV

Making patterns: Importance of accuracy — variation of sizes of sides and panels — treatment of differing materials — main types of foundation frames — popular shapes — patterns for "Empire" covers — curved panel patterns — patterns for fluted lampshade covers — formula for any-size fluted covers.

No matter how carefully a lampshade may be prepared and assembled, unless the pattern used when marking and cutting the covering material to shape is absolutely accurate the lampshade will not be a success. When cutting out the material for covering a shade, it is a great mistake to try to work without a pattern. You will save yourself a great deal of time and avoid wasting materials if a really accurate pattern is made first.

However carefully the wire frames have been made, there may be slight differences in the size of the sides or panels; it is therefore necessary to cut a separate pattern for each panel to allow for these differences, or a main pattern can be used if it is carefully checked against each panel or side for variations of size before the material is cut. Either thick paper or thin card will make a good pattern. Mark round the pattern on the material with a pencil or chalk. A ball-point pen should not be used, as the ink will rub off the pattern on to the covering material and is very difficult to remove. Pattern-making calls for great attention to detail. A very small error can result in a great deal of wasted material, to say nothing of wasted time.

It is a fairly simple matter to make patterns for panelled frames, but not quite so easy to make patterns for one-piece covers or fluted or pleated covers. When commencing to cut a pattern, first consider the material you are going to use. Generally speaking, soft materials are stitched to the frame, and allowance for turning and stitching must be made when cutting out the sides or panels. Stiff materials are cut to the exact size required for thonging or stitching to foundation frames.

There are two main types of lampshade frames—one with supporting side wires which divide the frame into panels, the other consisting of two wire shapes, one for the top and one for the bottom of the shade, which are used when the covering material is stiff enough to support the shade. If the wires of the frame are quite straight and even, it is a simple task to mark out the pattern

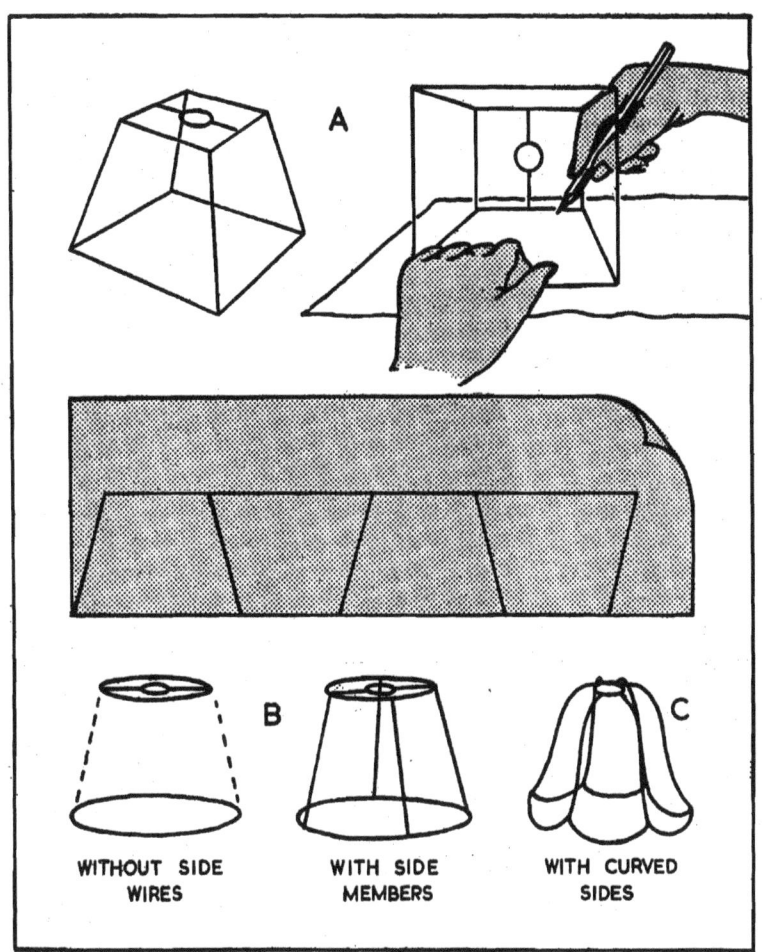

FIG. II. POPULAR FRAME SHAPES

from the frame measurements, but it is more difficult to make an accurate pattern when the wires are curved or round, such as for an "Empire" type shade. The illustration Fig. 11 shows some of the most popular shaped frames.

Fig. 11a is a small square frame suitable for a wall lamp, a chandelier or a very small table lamp, such as is used on a bedside table or dressing table. A pattern for this type of frame can be drawn directly on to a piece of stiff card. Fig. 11 shows how the pattern is drawn to the exact size, and placed on the material so as to avoid any waste. The pattern is the exact size required, and is suitable for use when cutting materials such as parchment, "Crinothene," etc. However, if a soft material is being used, about $\frac{1}{4}$ in. must be allowed all round the panels for turnings. If several frames are to be covered, a template may be cut in thin plywood or metal. In this case it will be necessary to test the pattern on each panel before starting to cut out the material, so that any variations, no matter how slight, may be allowed for. If chalk is used for marking out your pattern, keep the end well sharpened, as too broad an outline can make quite a considerable difference to the shade.

Fig. 11*b* shows an "Empire" type frame which can be made in any size, with or without side wires. In either case the covering material is best made in one piece. The diagram Fig. 12 shows how to draw a pattern and may be used for any size frame, ranging from very small candle size to large standard-lamp shades. There are two main points to the diagram—the elevation of the frame which is shown in the diagram in black, and the pattern which you will find heavily outlined. To make a pattern in this way it is necessary to draw an absolutely true elevation of the lampshade frame. Start with a large piece of paper, as it requires quite a lot of space, and at the bottom of the sheet of paper draw the elevation. This means making a drawing of the wire frame as it appears at eye level, and the drawing must be full size. Next draw a vertical line through the centre of the elevation up to the top of the sheet of paper. This line is marked 2—2 in the diagram. Draw a second line by continuing the left side line of the elevation to the top of the sheet; this is marked 3—3 in the illustration.

Now join the top right corner of the elevation with the line 2—2 by drawing an arc with the junctions of 2—2 and 3—3 as the axis. Draw a second arc from the lower right corner of the elevation to line 2—2, again taking the junction of lines 2 and 3 as the axis, draw a quarter circle from the lower left corner of the elevation down to line A below the elevation, and mark off the quarter circle into four equal divisions. Set compasses to any of the four divisions of the quarter circle, and mark off this distance four times from the junction of line 3 and the outer arc. Set the compasses again from the junction of line 3 and the outer arc to the fourth mark previously made on the outer arc, and mark off

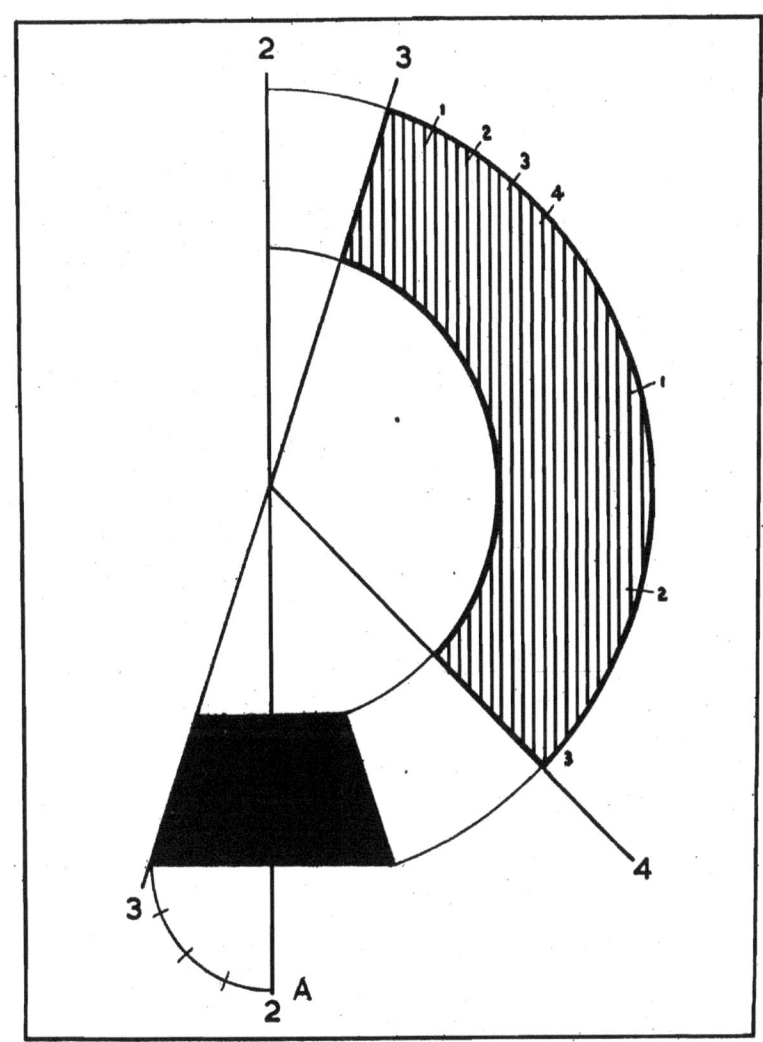

FIG. 12. PATTERN FORMULA

three times. Draw a line from the last mark to the junction of lines 2 and 3; this is line 4 in the diagram. The section of the arc falling between lines 3 and 4, and marked in stripes, is the pattern.

Try the pattern round the wire frame before cutting or marking the material. This method should produce an absolutely accurate

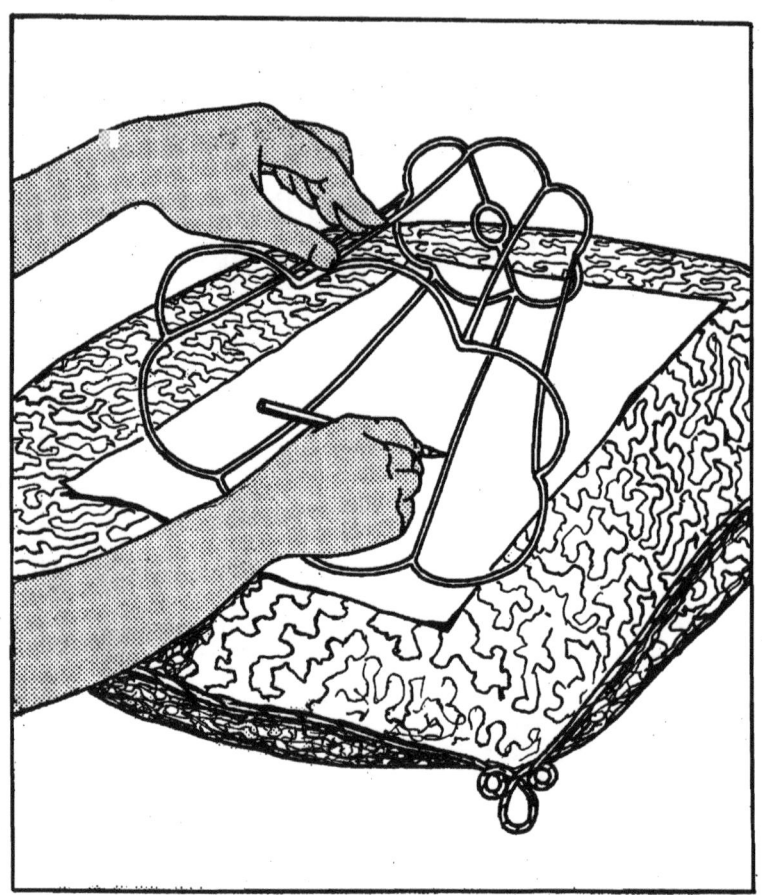

FIG. 13. SHAPED PATTERNS

pattern, but if the frame is to be covered with stiff material, thonged to the frame, allowance must be made for the seam where the two ends meet—about $\frac{1}{2}$ in. is usually sufficient. Patterns are best cut from stiff cardboard, or from wood or metal if you require to cover several shades of a kind. In either case it is essential that they be cut with a very sharp knife or scissors, so that the edges are cut clean.

Patterns for lampshades with curved panels, such as the one illustrated in Fig. 11c, can be made by placing a piece of fairly stiff card or paper on a pillow or cushion. Place a piece of stout paper on top of the card, then press the frame against the paper with enough pressure to make the shaped panel rest firmly on the paper, so that the outline of the panel can be marked in pencil. This is illustrated in Fig. 13. Patterns made by this method must be tried against every panel of the wire frame before cutting the material. Patterns should be cut to the exact size of the panels where a stiff material is to be used for the covering; but if it is intended to use a soft material, an allowance of at least ¼ in. all round the panel will be needed to allow for turnings.

An alternative method for making patterns for curved panels is to place a piece of thin tracing paper over the panel of the frame, and press over the wires until the shape of the panel is impressed on it. Take the paper from the frame and cut round the impression. Try against the wire frame, and if quite accurate place on thin card and trace round it for your pattern.

One of the easiest types of shade for which to cut a pattern is the fluted cover. Fig. 14 gives the measurements for cutting a

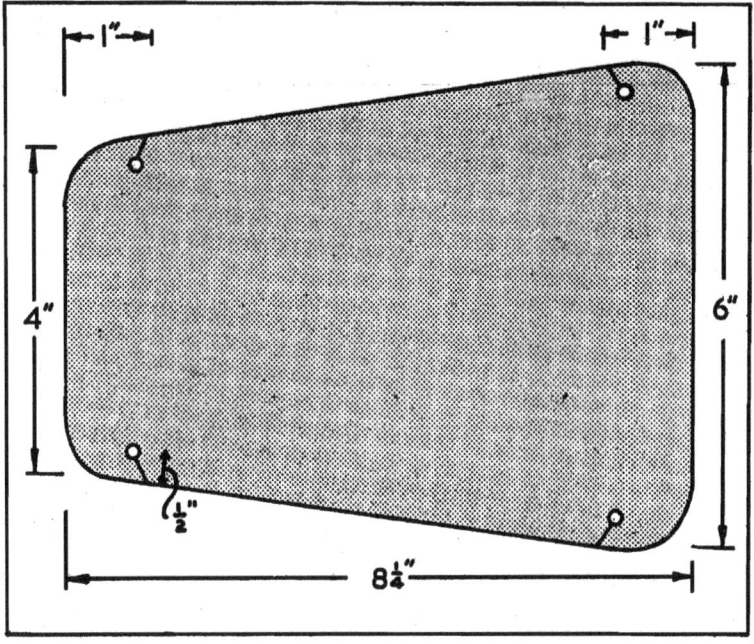

FIG. 14. FLUTED PATTERNS

fluted shade. This type of shade is made on a two-piece wire foundation. The flutes are joined by stitching or stapling. Only a stiff material is suitable for this type of cover. The flutes may be made any size, and any number of flutes may be used for the cover, according to the size of the foundation frame. The fluted shade illustrated has eight flutes. The top ring of the frame is 5 in. in diameter and the bottom ring is 8 in. Cut a pattern from the diagram given and place on the material, reversing for each flute to save wastage of covering material. Cut the flutes and punch four small holes in each, as shown in the diagram. Now make a diagonal cut from the centre of each punched hole to the edge of the flute as shown. The flutes are joined by stitching or by wire staples along a stitch line marked ¼ in. from the edge. The wire frames are pressed through the diagonal slits into the punched holes and the edges of the flutes stitched to the frame where they meet. The flutes may be edged with a decorative braid to complete the shade.

The pattern measurements given in Fig. 14 are suitable only for use with a frame of the dimensions given. Patterns for fluted covers for other sizes of frames are quite easy to make. First decide the number of flutes and the depth of shade you wish to make. The cover can consist of more than eight flutes, or if you wish you can have fewer, although this will cause your flutes to have rather a flat appearance.

Take the bottom ring of the frame and mark this off in equal divisions according to the number of flutes you have decided to have in the shade. Cut a rectangle in stiff card, curve this and hold it against one of the divisions of the base ring. If the curve is too pronounced, trim one side of the card as necessary until you are satisfied that the curve gives a pleasing effect. However, should the curve prove too shallow you will have to cut a wider piece of card. The base of the flute is wider than the top. After cutting away any surplus from the card, round off the corners to neaten the flute, mark the positions where you are going to punch the holes and cut diagonal lines, and the pattern is ready for use.

A fluted shade made with top and bottom rings the same size is very attractive on some lamps, such as a hanging lamp. In this case the pattern for the flutes will be the same size top and bottom. Although this type of pattern is easy to make, a little care in the making of the pattern goes a long way towards making a faultless shade.

CHAPTER V

Simple lampshades: A thonged pendant shade — checking the frame — binding — pattern making — marking and cutting the material — punching the thong holes — thonging — sequence of work — use of plastic thonging. Covering an "Empire" frame — material — inspection — binding the frame — making the pattern — attaching the cover.

THIS chapter deals with the making of two very simple lampshades. The frame of the first one described is illustrated in Fig. 15. It has a square top and a slightly larger square base. The side members are straight, dividing the frame into four panels. This type of frame is obtainable in small sizes suitable for wall lamps or bedside table lamps, up to large standard-lamp sizes. The very small sizes can be had with a fitting known as a "Butterfly" (see Fig. 15). These are shaped wires which fit over the electric-light bulb, and thus enable one to set the shade at any angle.

However, the lampshade described in this chapter is an average-

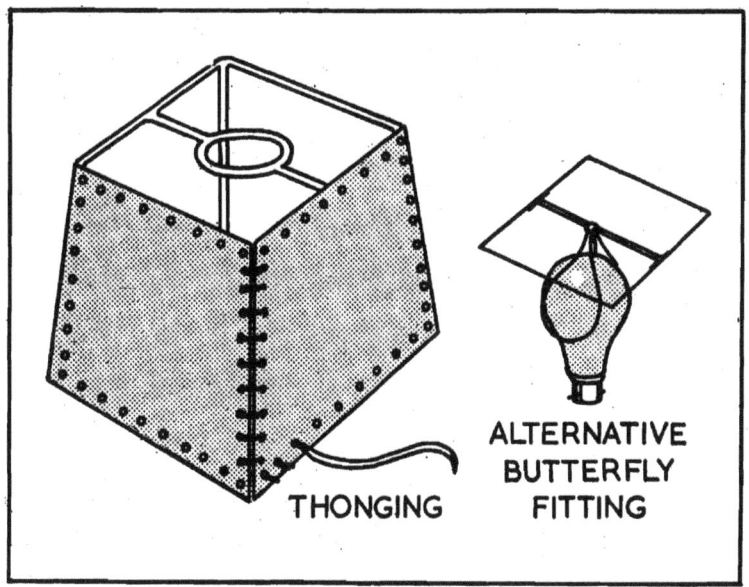

FIG. 15. THONGED COVER

sized pendant with a gimbal at the top, with a thonged cover. When starting to make a shade, the very first thing to do is to examine carefully all the wires, straightening any which may be bent and removing any rust which may be present. Following this simple rule can make a tremendous difference to the shade, as even a very slightly bent wire will prevent your making an accurate panel, while the presence of rust could discolour the inside of the shade.

As this is to be a thonged lampshade, the wires may either be painted to match or contrast with the covering material, or they can be covered with bias binding to match the covering material or the thonging. Bind the frame carefully with tight, slightly overlapping spirals of binding. When you come to a corner, go very carefully to avoid forming bulky joins. Fasten the ends of the bias binding with a fabric adhesive or by sewing. But whichever method is used, make very certain that the binding is securely fastened. Cover all the frame with binding, except the gimbal fitting.

The next stage is to make the pattern. Do not be tempted to save time by marking the shape of the side panels directly on to the material. It is a bad habit to get into when making lampshades, and really it is much more economical in time and covering material to make a well-fitting pattern first. Pattern making is most important, and great care should be paid to this part of the craft.

To make the pattern, take your bound or painted frame and place it on a piece of stiff paper or thin card. With a pencil, mark round one of the side panels. Next cut the panel pattern very carefully. Cut just outside the pencil lines, *not* inside. Test this pattern on each of the four panels. If each of the panels is not completely accurate with the pattern, make a note to make due allowance for these differences when marking and cutting out the covering material. Before marking the covering material it is as well to try the pattern on the material in various ways, to avoid waste in cutting out. It is surprising what a small quantity of material is required to cover a shade if this rule is kept. With straight-panelled frames of this type, the most economical way of placing the pattern is shown in Fig. 16. There is hardly any waste at all. Of course, cover patterns for all frames do not work out so conveniently—such as those with curved panels, for example—but generally time spent at this stage is well worth while.

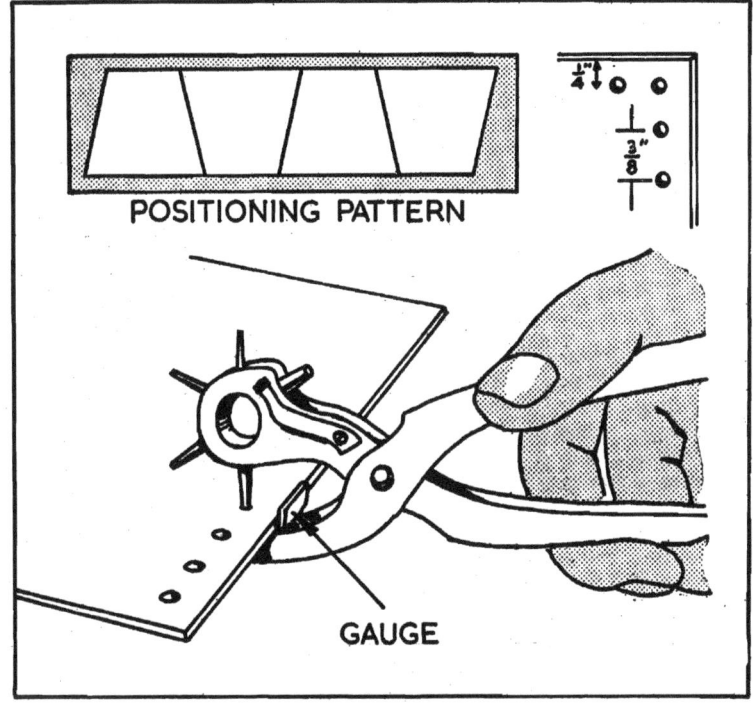

FIG. 16. PLACING PATTERNS

The simple lampshade shape shown can be covered in parchment. This material is obtainable in several qualities and surface patterns and also in several colours. Do not choose the most inexpensive quality: the heavier ones do not tear easily and are, therefore, much easier to work with.

Choose a firm flat surface for use when marking out your pattern. Place the parchment on it and mark round the pattern with pencil. Parchment is easily marked with a lead pencil. Mark out all the four panels, not forgetting to allow for any slight differences in shape or size. Then cut out the material, using a pair of sharp scissors or a razor blade guided by a straight-edge.

Now the next step is to punch the thonging holes all round each of the panels. It is essential for the good appearance of the finished shade that these holes are carefully punched and at equal distances apart. They should be cut at a distance of about $\frac{1}{4}$ in. from the edge and about $\frac{3}{8}$ in. from each other (see Fig. 16).

Choose a punch size which will give a hole big enough to take the thonging but no bigger. Lightly mark the position of the holes on the parchment, or use a gauge such as the one illustrated in Fig. 16. If you are using a six-way revolving-head punch of the type illustrated in Fig. 16, all the panels may be cut at the same time. It is essential that the same number of holes are punched in each panel. There should be no difficulty in punching through the four panels together when the shade is being covered with parchment. The four panels are best held together with a strong paper clip while the holes are punched.

Should the punch being used have become worn and the holes therefore not cut cleanly, place a piece of thin cord over the anvil of the punch, and it will be found that the holes can then be cut quite cleanly.

The panels must now be thonged to the shade. As the shade is being covered with parchment there is no right or wrong side of material; but when using material such as "Crinothene," care should be taken to ensure that the right side of the material is placed on the outside of the shade. The amount of thonging for a lampshade is about three times the total length of the wires. A more attractive appearance results if the width of the thonging is in keeping with the size of the frame. Never use a heavy wide thonging on a small frame, or a dainty narrow one on a large frame.

Commence at one of the top corners by tying one end of the thonging material to one of the wires of the frame. Take two of the panels which have been cut out in parchment, and commencing at the top of the shade secure the sides of both panels to the upright side wires at one of the corners. Pass the thonging from the back of the panels through the second hole down from the top, bring it to the front, and pass it through the coinciding hole of the adjoining panel, over the back of the corner side wire, and through the next hole down in the first panel, as illustrated in Fig. 17.

Continue thonging down to the second hole from the bottom in each panel. Now cut the thonging about $\frac{3}{4}$ in. from the panel and work the end under the tight thonging inside the lampshade. Release the knot first tied at the top of the shade, cut off any surplus thonging, and tuck the end under inside the tight thonging in the same way. First thong the panels over all the side members of the panels, then thong right round the top of the shade with

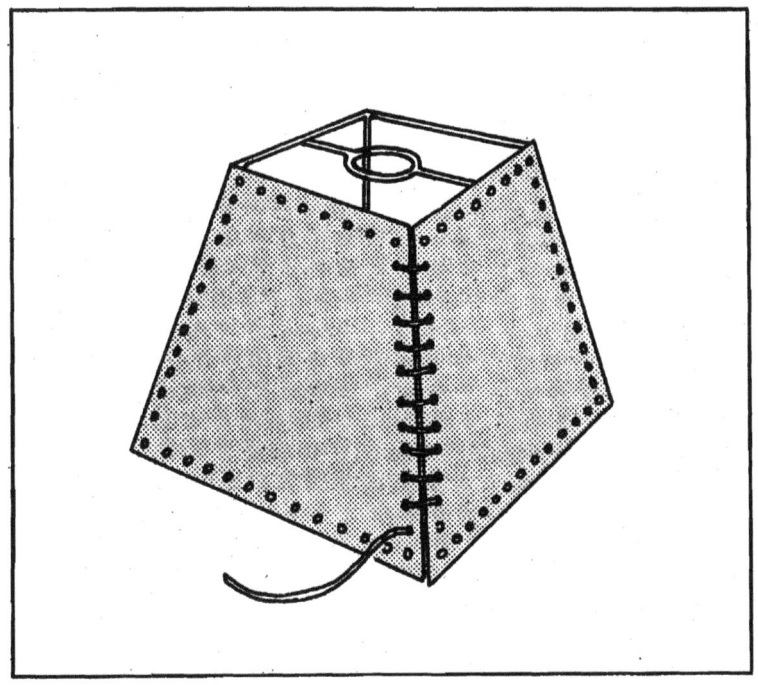

FIG. 17. THONGING

a single length of thonging. Lastly, thong round the bottom of the shade, making sure that all the ends of the thonging are securely tucked out of sight under the thonging inside the shade.

When thonging parchment, care must be taken not to pull the thonging too tight, as if undue strain is placed on the edges of the parchment it may split and break. The thonging need be pulled just tightly enough to hold the material to the frame. Consideration of this becomes very important when using plastic thonging, as some types stretch when warm and shrink as they become cold. The warmth of the hands when handling the thonging may be sufficient to stretch the plastic, and if it is pulled too tightly, when it shrinks it will split the edges of the parchment.

A simple "Empire" type frame without side members is used as the foundation of the next shade described. For this you will need a small ring approximately 5 in. across, fitted with a gimbal, and a larger bottom ring, probably about 8 in. to 10 in. across, without a gimbal. Again, parchment is described as the covering material, but any stiff material is suitable, such as "Crinothene," Acetate, buckram, etc. The material used must be stiff enough to support the shape of the shade, as there are no side members.

To make the lampshade, first inspect the wire rings, making sure that they are not bent out of shape at all and that there is no rust on them. Next, as previously described, paint or bind the rings. If you are binding them, use bias binding wound spirally and slightly overlapping all round each ring, with the exception of the gimbal. Finish off by sticking the end with adhesive or by a few stitches with matching thread. Using the method and diagram shown and described in the chapter on pattern making, mark out in stiff paper or thin card a pattern.

First draw a true elevation of the lampshade at the foot of a large sheet of paper. The elevation must be full size. The width at the top should equal the diameter of the top ring of the frame, and the bottom of the elevation drawn on the sheet of paper should be equal to the diameter of the bottom ring of the shade. As a guide to the suitable height for the shade, add the diameters of the top and bottom rings of the frame and divide the total by two. For instance, if the top ring is 5 in. and the diameter of the bottom ring is 8 in., this gives a total of 13 in., so a suitable height for the shade would be $6\frac{1}{2}$ in. This must be taken as a guide only, and the size of the lampstand, or if pendant the size of the room, should also be considered. After drawing the elevation of the shade, draw a straight line extending the left side of the elevation. Draw a second line vertically through the elevation in the centre. From the axis where these lines meet draw an arc from the bottom left corner of the elevation to the top of the paper. To complete the pattern outline, take the largest ring and roll it along the arc. Mark the ring with chalk at the starting-point, and also mark the paper at the starting-point. Mark again when the mark on the frame reaches the line. From that point draw a line to the axis. This is illustrated in Fig. 12.

Place it on the parchment (with this type of frame there is bound to be some wastage in cutting, but the pieces can probably be utilized to make a panelled shade). Make an allowance for overlapping seam. Test the cover on the frame, and if you are certain it is an accurate fit, mark out the thonging holes all round the bottom and top edges.

Commence the thonging at the top edge by tying the thonging material to the wire, then work round the top ring, finishing the ends as was described for the previous shade, by putting them neatly under the thonging inside the shade. Now join the side seam, which may either be stuck with adhesive or, if preferred, holes can be punched and threaded through with the thonging. Then thong in the same way round the bottom of the shade. Make sure that the thonging lies in the same direction round the bottom ring as it does round the top one.

These two frames are the simplest ones to cover, but there is great variety in the manner in which they can be covered, and when covered in fabric and daintily trimmed they look anything but simple. The lampshade maker is well advised to explore and learn thoroughly the many ways in which these two shapes can be covered, before attempting the more difficult, curved types of frame.

CHAPTER VI

Lampshades with stitched covers: Bed-lamp shade — preparation — choice of material — making patterns — stitching — decoration. Another bed-lamp shade — inspecting the frame — binding — sewing — attaching net frill. Standard-lamp shade — curved and rounded panels — checking the frame — binding — thonging and stitching — decoration.

AFTER making simple thonged shades, the worker can progress to other kinds. The next type of lampshade described has a stitched cover, and this is no more difficult to make than a thonged shade. For this type of lampshade one of the plastics such as "Crinothene" or "Rilfoil" can be used. The shade chosen to illustrate this method is a bed-lamp shade, which is made on one of the standard-style frames which are obtainable from all handicraft dealers.

The preparation for making a stitched cover is much the same as for thonged covers. Commence by examining the frame for rust and bends in the wire. Slight rust can be removed by rubbing hard with a pad of newspaper, and do not be tempted to leave the rust on the frame, as it may come through the cover later and ruin the shade. With stitched covers it is always necessary to bind the frames with bias binding. It is not enough to paint them, as the stitching is done through the binding and it is then finally covered with gimp. This serves two purposes—it covers the joints in the shade and serves to decorate the lampshade.

The lampshade illustrated in Fig. 18 is a shade for a bed-lamp, and in making it there is one extra point to be considered. It is a common fault amongst lampshade workers to make small lampshades with the top completely covered in. This is a bad fault, as in these small shades the bulb is of necessity nearly touching the shade, and the heat from it, in an enclosed space, will cause the covering material to scorch, singe or melt, according to the type being used.

To overcome this, the shade must be designed to allow a small part at the back or top to be left open, to allow the hot air generated by the heat from the bulb to escape. In the case of the lampshade illustrated, it is obvious that the top must be covered in one piece with the front, then the two sides. The part between the two wires at the back, just below the hook, is left uncovered, thus leaving a space for the escape of the heat.

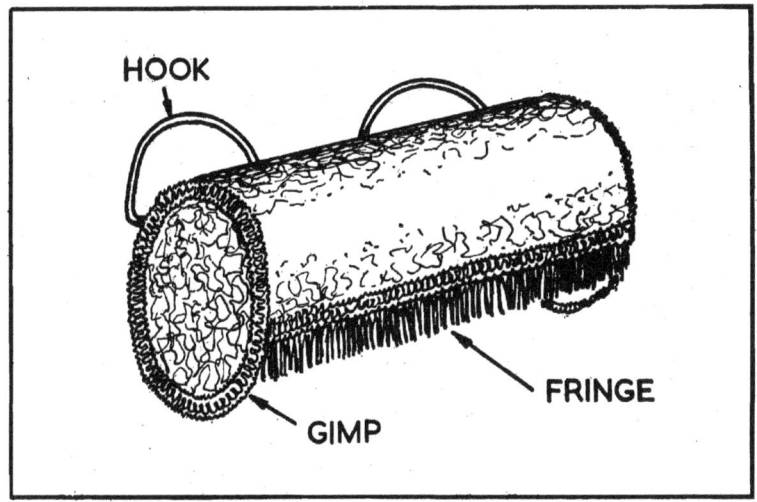

FIG. 18. BED-LAMP

To make the lampshade, first inspect all the wires and then bind the frame as previously described. Cover all the wires except the gimbal ring.

As this lamp is to be used on a bedhead, choose a soft, restful colour for the "Crinothene," something which will suggest comfortable relaxation—warm peach or amber, decorated with gimp and a small fringe. The parts of this frame are quite small, and if the worker has off-cuts of "Crinothene" at hand it may be possible to combine two colours, one for the top piece and one for the side pieces.

Make the patterns after inspecting and binding the frame with bias binding. In this case it will be quite a simple matter to make patterns for the three pieces—one for the top, which reaches from the front wire to the top back wire by the hook, and two circles to fit the ends, which are closed in completely. Take careful measurements and cut out in stiff card or thick paper—even with such simple shapes as these it is inadvisable to mark directly on to the covering material. Try the patterns against the frame to ensure that they are accurate, then place the patterns on the material, mark round them with chalk, and cut the parts neatly to shape.

Commence stitching the cover to the frame with one of the side

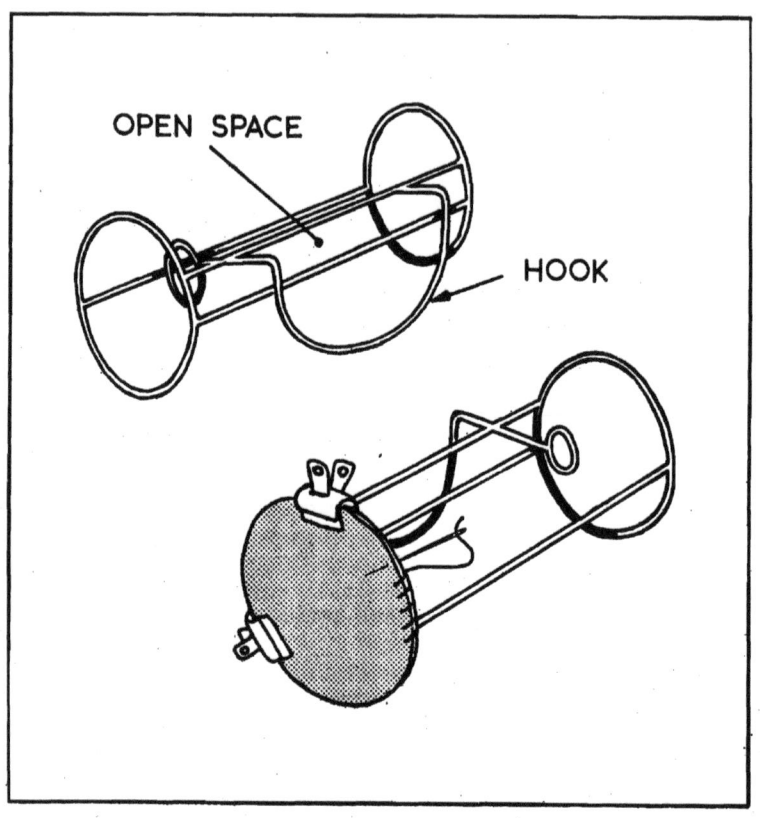

FIG. 19. SEWING " CRINOTHENE "

panels. Place the panel on the bound wire, and with a needle threaded with strong matching cotton stitch the panel to the bias binding, and stitch right round the edge of the circle. When sewing "Crinothene" care must be taken not to allow the covering material to move, and to prevent this one or two paper clips can be used, as shown in Fig. 19, to keep the panel in place. Every care must be taken not to buckle the panel while stitching it in place, and it is at this stage that the value of cutting accurate patterns becomes apparent. If pattern making has not been absolutely accurate the panel may turn out to be a little too small or a little too large, and "Crinothene", which has little elasticity, may not stretch to fill gaps caused by poor pattern making.

The thread used for sewing the cover to the bound wires should match the covering material, for although it will not show on the outside it will be seen from the inside.

"Crinothene" is quite easy to sew with a medium fine sewing needle, but "Rilfoil," which may be used as an alternative covering, requires a slightly larger needle to go through easily. The stitch line with both these materials should be about $\frac{1}{8}$ in. to $\frac{1}{4}$ in. in from the edge of the material, but it may be a little more, and it is best not to make more than eight stitches to the inch. If more than eight stitches are made to each inch, it may weaken the material at the edges. As "Crinothene" is fairly easily pierced with a sewing needle, there is no need to punch stitch holes, though this can be done if desired—with a sharp-pointed bradawl —before commencing stitching.

After the first side panel has been stitched into place on the lampshade frame, fit the other round panel to the opposite end and stitch it firmly into place.

Care should be taken while stitching not to pull the cotton too tightly, as a strong cotton may tear the covering material if pulled too tightly. With the ends attached fit and stitch the main panel, which reaches from the front wire over the top of the frame to the first wire at the back. This completes the actual stitching of the frame, which will need decorating to finish.

As this lamp is for use in a bedroom, the decoration can be a little more fancy than those of a living-room lampshade, and the choice of colour will depend largely upon the room in which the bed-lamp is to be used. The lampshade illustrated is decorated with gimp and fringe. When making this particular shade it will be necessary to stitch the fringe along the bottom of the shade first. One piece of fringe may be used. The gimp is attached next. This should be of a suitable colour to tone with the covering material, and it should be wide enough to fold over the stitched seams of the shade and completely cover the joins and stitches. Take a length of gimp and place it over one corner of the lampshade. Using cotton of a suitable colour, commence stitching at the top of the shade and work downwards, sewing the gimp neatly and firmly in place. Stitch gimp along the two long edges, then sew it round the two ends. When stitching gimp, sew through the "Crinothene" and the bias binding, and sew along both edges of the gimp. Do not make the mistake of sewing over the wires inside the frame, as this spoils the look of the finished shade.

The next shade to be described is also for a bed-lamp, and this lampshade consists of three panels and a back piece, as illustrated in Fig. 20. The gimbal is at the top of the shade.

The style of shade is very suitable for using two colours of covering materials. The back and front panels can be done in cream and the petal-shaped panels in deep rose. The lampshade would be best trimmed with a box-pleated frill of double net in a matching rose colour.

As in previous instructions, commence by carefully inspecting the wire frame for any faults in the construction and for rust. It should be emphasized here that these frames are not usually faulty—indeed, if bought from a reputable firm they are generally very accurate and completely free from rust; but it may sometimes happen that corresponding panels vary in size by a very slight degree. Therefore it can save a great deal of wasted material

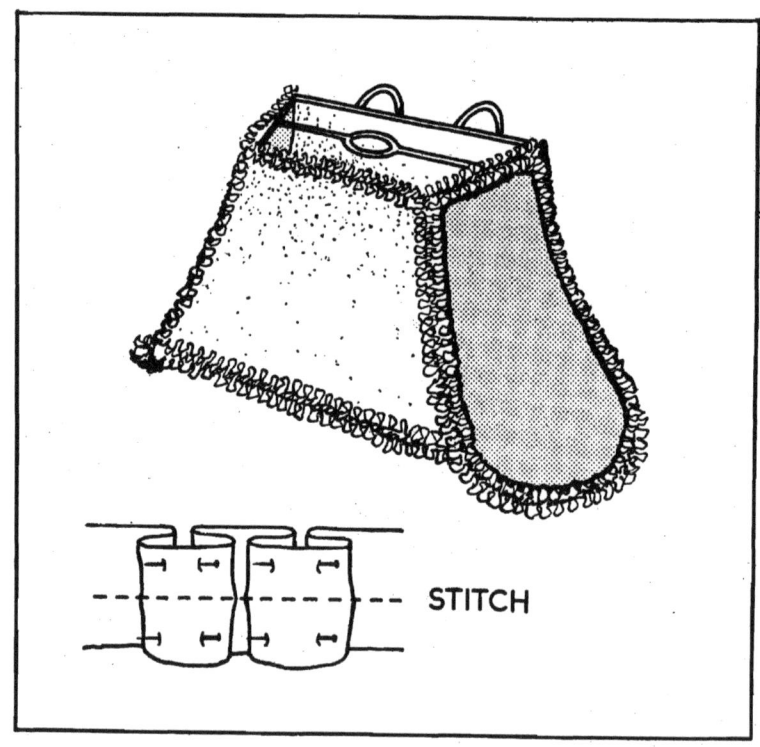

FIG. 20. ANOTHER BED-LAMP

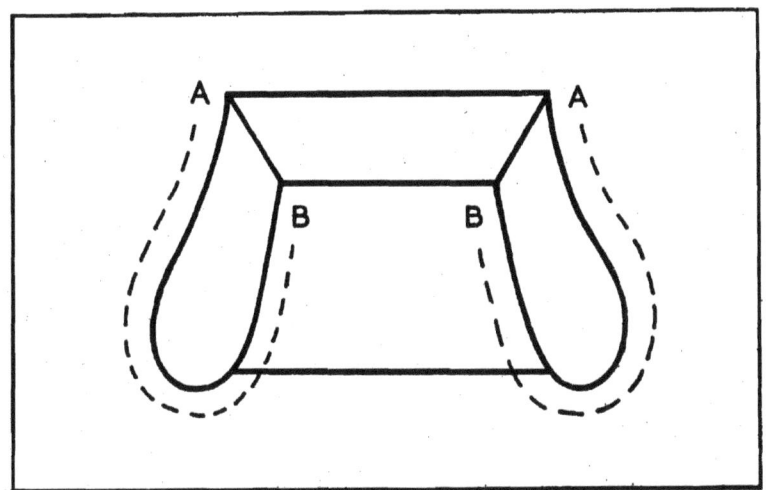

FIG. 21. DECORATING A BED-LAMP

if this simple check is made when commencing to make a lampshade.

Bind the wire frame with bias binding. In this shade, as the two main panels are rose, the binding should be of the same colour. When making a two-coloured frame it is usually best to match the binding to the predominating colour.

Take time and trouble over binding the frame to ensure that it is tight and smooth, with no lumpy corners, then make the pattern. As the panels of this shade are covered at the ends, though still flat across, the best way of marking the pattern to shape is to use the frame itself. Rub white chalk over the bound wires on the outside of the shade, then press a panel on brown paper or cardboard.

Commence by stitching the back panel to the frame; in this particular shade the top is left open and the back is completely filled in. Stitch the front panel to the frame, then attach the two petal-shaped panels.

To make the frill, two lengths of net about three times the total length of wires to be covered (*e.g.*, the measurements of the two petal panels, plus right round the top of the shade, plus across the front wire) will be required (see Fig. 20). Place the pieces of net one on top of the other and pin into box pleats right along the length of the net, as illustrated in Fig. 20. Stitch through the middle of the pleats, remove the pins, and stitch or stick with white adhesive a piece of the frill across the bottom front wire, then a piece round each petal panel from A to B, as shown in Fig. 21. To finish, put the remaining piece around the top. If additional decoration is required, add a very narrow gimp down the centre of the frill.

The next stitched lampshade, shown in Fig. 22, is for a large standard lamp and is slightly more difficult to make than those previously described, because of the curved and rounded panels and because, being a large frame with many panels, it is a little

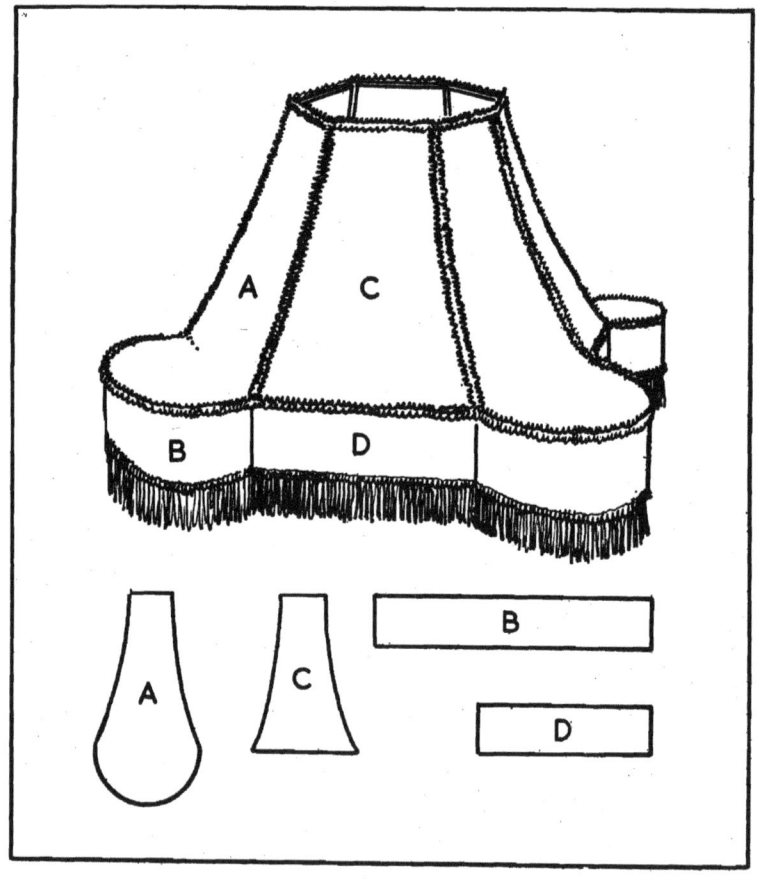

FIG. 22. STANDARD LAMPSHADE

more difficult to handle while making. There are four different shapes in the panels, and the shade is made up of sixteen panels altogether. In Fig. 22 the panel shapes are marked A, B, C and D.

Commence, as always in lampshade making, by checking the wire frame. In a shade of this size it is advisable to go further and check the joints in the wire frame. It is unlikely that there will be any fault in them, as the best manufacturers make their frames with strong, well-finished spot-welded joints.

Next bind all the wires of the frame with bias binding. In a many-panelled shade such as this it will take thought and care to avoid lumpy corners. The best sequence of work will be to bind down the curved side and down the small upright wires, finishing each end with a few stitches. Continue by binding right round the top wire, next right round the two bottom wires. In this way you will avoid going over the same corner too many times.

In the shade illustrated both thonging and stitching have been employed. The upright sides of the panels are thonged, and the top and bottom edges stitched and covered with gimp. The thonging used and the gimp should be an exact match in colour.

After covering the frame with bias binding, place it against a sheet of strong paper and place both paper and frame on a soft cushion or pillow, press the frame well down into the cushion, and the paper will then take on the shape of the panel (see Fig. 13). Draw round the outline of the panel on the paper. Cut the pattern out and test it against the other panels of the same shape. Make patterns for the other panel parts in the same way.

Punch thonging holes along the edges of the panel to be thonged, making certain that the holes in neighbouring panels coincide. Thong the panels into position, then stitch along the tops of all the panels and along the two bottom wires.

Cover all the stitched edges with gimp, either sewn or stuck on. If a fringe is required on these large frames, try a double one, made by using two lengths of fringe each a different colour and length. For instance, have a fringe matching the "Crinothene," about 3 in. deep, and another fringe about 2 in. deep to match the gimp. Use the small fringe over the longer one, so that the two colours mingle.

CHAPTER VII

Fabric-covered lampshades: Materials — binding the frame — making the pattern — covering the frame — trimming. A bowl-shaped shade. Another method of making fabric-covered lampshades. Novelty methods — using lace or net over stiff paper.

THIS chapter deals with the making of fabric-covered lampshades. Fabric lampshade covers are quite easy to make if the directions are carefully followed and the correct sequence of work is observed.

There are very many fabrics suitable for covering lampshades— in fact, any material that does not completely block out light can be used as a covering, but loosely woven materials are difficult to use, as they do not hold the stitches very well.

There are several methods by which fabric lampshades are made, and it is a matter of choice which method is adopted. In some cases the shape of the frame will indicate a particular method.

When making a fabric lampshade the panels may be covered separately, or several panels may be covered together, or again the cover can be made in one piece for attachment to the frame.

The lampshade shown in Fig. 23 illustrates a method by which fabric covers can be made to fit simply shaped frames of any size. The illustration shows a medium-sized pendant shade in which all the panels curve inwards. Usually it will be found that lampshade frames with concave panels (inward curving) are generally more suitable for covering with fabric than are frames with convex (outward curving) panels.

As when making other shades, the wire frame must be checked carefully and any bent wires straightened out. Rust spots can be removed by rubbing with a pad of newspaper, or if very bad, with emery paper. Check for any broken joints, and when this has been done bind the frame with bias binding in the manner previously described. The binding may alternatively be done with strips of the covering material, and if this is done cut strips of material about 1 in. in width. Fold over and press one edge of the strips; it is not necessary to fold over both edges, as the other raw edge is covered by the overlapping folded edge while binding the frame. If the covering material is thick it will be found best

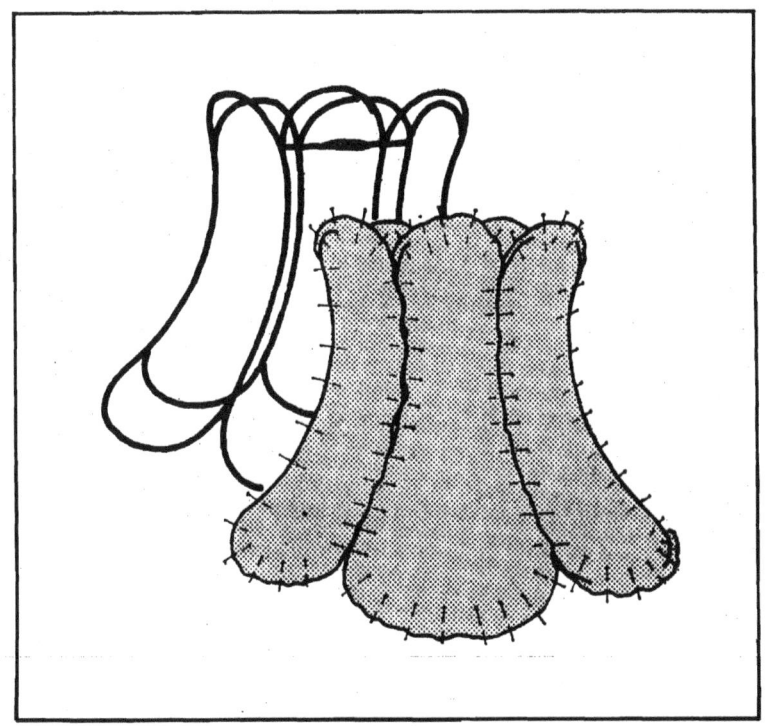

FIG. 23. FABRIC COVER

to use bias binding; but whatever binding is used, the frame must be bound tightly and carefully, avoiding lumps and awkward joins, as these may show under a fabric cover.

When covering a shade in the manner shown in Fig. 23, first bind all the side wires, then bind round the top and finish round the bottom. When making fabric-covered lampshades it is most important to remember that the covering material must *always* be used on the cross or bias, so that the stretch is even in all directions. For first attempts at lampshade making choose an easy-to-handle material, such as washing satin or one of the cotton crêpes.

Fig. 24 illustrates a very quick and easy way of covering a lampshade. This is not strictly a professional method, but it gives very good results. This method is not suitable for all shapes of frames, but works very well on those with several straight panels. The shade illustrated is one of the ready-made frames which can be obtained from most handicraft dealers. It has a base of about 12 in. diameter and is suitable as a pendant or a table lamp. To cover this frame you will require a piece of material about 27 in. square; cut this diagonally across to form two triangles. This cover is made of two pieces which are joined with two side seams.

Make a rough paper pattern of half the frame. The pattern need not be exact, as adjustments can be made when stitching the cover. Lay the pattern on the two triangles of material, which should be placed together, and tack very carefully down both sides of the pattern and the pieces of material. Take the material and pattern and slip over the frame. Pin down the side seams, keeping the material very taut (see Fig. 24). Remove the cover from the frame, and machine-stitch or back-stitch along the side seams about $\frac{1}{4}$ in. away from the pins. This is done to allow for french seams. Cut away all surplus material from the sides only, but do not cut the top or bottom of the material.

A french seam is useful in making lampshades, as it will hide raw edges, and materials which are likely to fray will be protected at the seam edges. After machining down the seam on the right side of the material (about $\frac{1}{4}$ in. from the pins marking the position of the finished seam), trim off any surplus material wrong side out, and pin or tack the seam, making sure that the raw edges of the first seam are folded inside the second line of stitching, and sew along the seam at the position of the first set of pins.

It is very necessary that the covering should be taut on the frame, and at this stage try the covering over the frame again and make adjustments necessary. When the side seams are satisfactory, put the covering back on the frame right side out, and pull it well down on the frame. Pin top and bottom of material to the bound wires at top and bottom of the shade, pulling very tightly before pinning to ensure that the material is completely free from wrinkles. Turn the material over the wires and with matching cotton stitch down all along, taking each stitch right over the wire. Cut away any surplus material. The shade is now ready for the trimming, and this particular lampshade is simply decorated with narrow gimp around top and bottom. Place the gimp so that it comes just over the edge of the wires and covers the stitches. This is the simplest form of fabric-covered shade.

The next method described is rather more professional and is used for every variety of shaped frame. To illustrate this method the making of a bowl shade to hang from the ceiling is described. These bowl-shaped frames are hung close to a ceiling to give a very pleasant diffused light. If expense is no object this type of frame may be covered in one piece, but it will require a very large

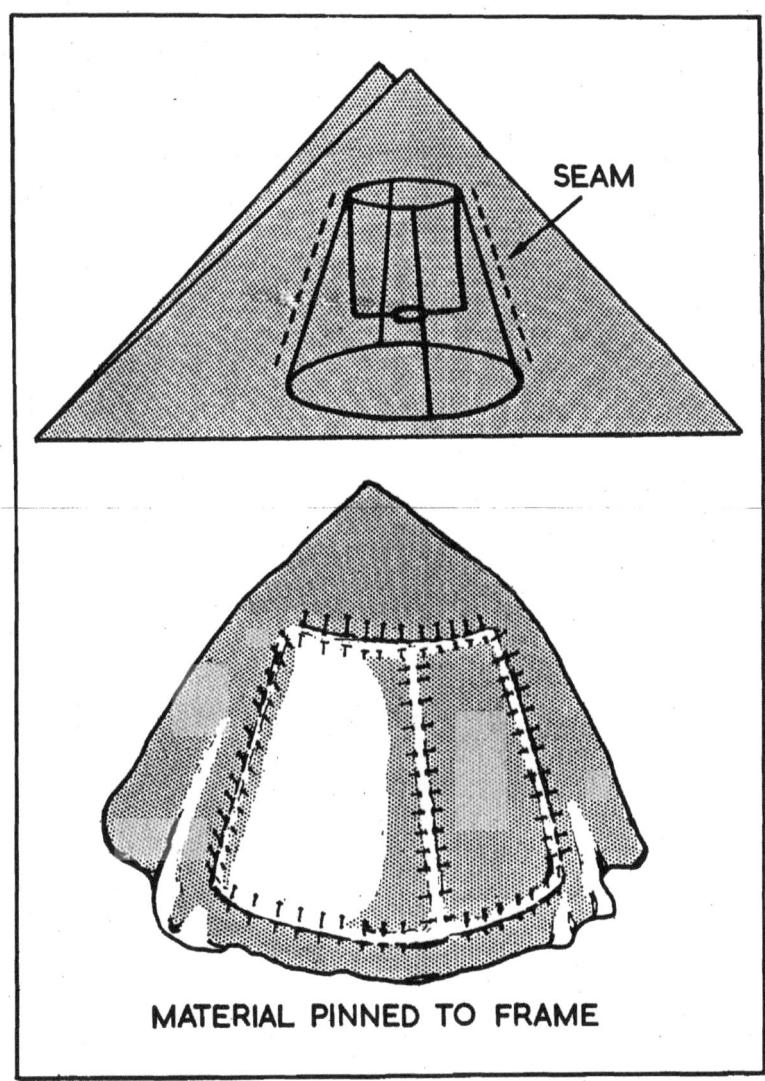

FIG. 24. QUICK AND EASY METHOD FOR FABRICS

piece of material to get it on the true bias, and it will be found more economical to cover it in two pieces.

The illustration Fig. 25 shows how the material is fitted over half the foundation by pinning it to the tape-bound edges of the frame. Commence by folding over one corner of the material to form a triangle which can then be cut off, to ensure that the material is used on the bias. This trimmed corner should be pinned parallel with the top of the frame when the cover is

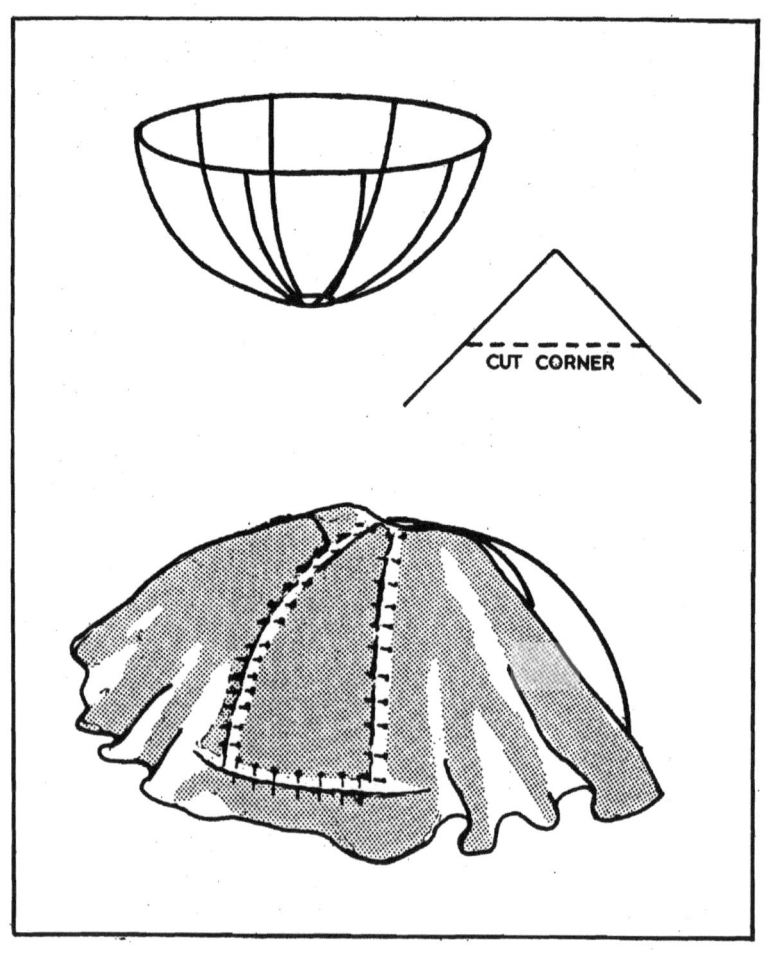

FIG. 25. FITTING MATERIAL

commenced. Using small steel pins, pin the material to the top wire of the frame, as shown in the illustration, commencing at the centre panel, then move to the bottom of the panel and pin that to the bound wire, keeping the material very taut, and using plenty of pins so that the material is held firmly and securely. The pins at top and bottom should all be vertical. After fastening the material at top and bottom, pin along one side edge, fastening the pins through the material and the binding over the wire frame. Pin all along one side very firmly, then pull and stretch the material well so that there are no wrinkles and it is really taut over the panel, then pin the second side very firmly to the frame.

Be generous with the use of pins, and place them all horizontally at the side edges. After pinning all sides, commence at a top corner, pulling the material tightly to shape, remove one pin at a time, then replace it after tightening the material. Work all round the panels in this way, removing a pin, pulling the material tight, and replacing the pin in position. Only by giving attention to this part of the work can you get a perfectly smooth cover with no sags or wrinkles and the strain even in all directions. After stitching and pinning the first panel, move round to the next one and repeat the tightening process. Pin the top first, then the bottom, next the side edge. Starting again at the top corner, remove the pins one by one, pull the material taut and replace the pins. When this has been done all round the second panel, go on to the panel on the other side of the first panel and repeat the process.

When the three panels have been covered and the material is evenly stretched and firmly pinned over the wires, trim away any surplus material to within $\frac{1}{2}$ in. to $\frac{1}{4}$ in. of the pins. Next thread an ordinary sewing needle with cotton or strong sewing silk of a colour to match the covering material. Sew along the top edge, first turning the material over, and sew through the folded material to the bound wire. Oversew the edges and remove the pins one at a time as progress is made. Never take out more than one or two pins at a time, or the tension of the material will relax. Sew firmly along the top edge, then down the left edge, removing only one or two pins at a time. Sew up the right side edge. While oversewing the edges of the cover, trim and neaten the edge as you go along. It is not necessary to sew along the other two wires dividing the three panels, and the pins holding these two wires may be removed after all the edges have been stitched.

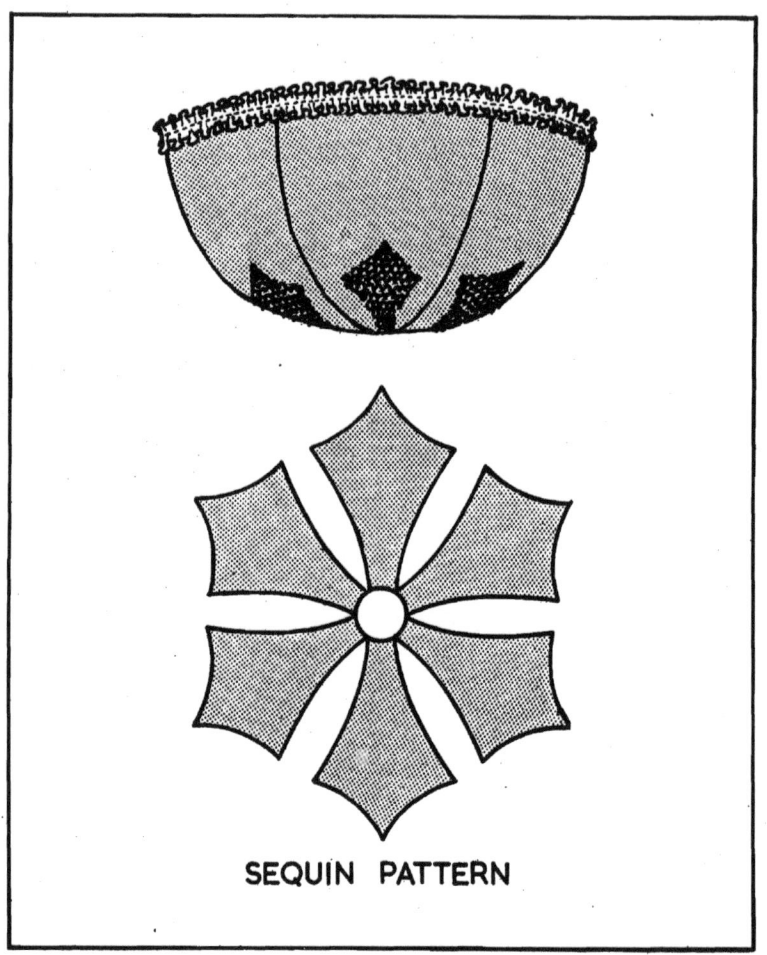

FIG. 26. DECORATING SHADES

The second half of the cover is made in the same way, by stretching the material on the bias over the remaining three panels, pinning round each panel as the work progresses to remove all sags, wrinkles and creases, and lastly stitching the edges to the tape-bound wires of the frame. It will be seen from this description of covering a lampshade how very important it is to bind the frame carefully and firmly. If the binding is loose in any place it will not stand up to the strain of the material, and the cover will develop sags where the weaknesses of the binding are.

When the covering has been completed the inside should be carefully inspected and any raw edges that show inside should be trimmed, but if the work has been carefully done from the beginning, and the edges of the material trimmed as they are oversewn, there should not be any ragged edges visible inside the frame.

If a thin material is being used to cover the frame it may need a lining, and this, if required, is fairly easy to fit. It is put into place in the same way as the cover, by stretching, pinning, tightening, trimming and stitching the lining material over the bound wires, exactly as for the cover, but in this case work from the inside of the shade. To save making bulky seams at the side wires when working the lining, make only two panels at a time, and so arrange the seams that they run along the side wires of the frame, to which the covering material will not be stitched.

The bowl-type frame illustrated could be trimmed in several ways—it could have gimp stitched along all the edges, with a tassel falling from the centre, or it could have ruching along the top wire edge and a gathered rosette arranged at the centre point where the wires meet.

The lampshade in Fig. 26 has, however, been decorated in a more ambitious style. The covering material is deep cream satin, and a rather wide ruching of the same material has been stitched along the top wire. Starting from the centre point, a pattern in gold-coloured sequins has been built up with a point going up each pattern—the illustration shows how the pattern is built up. Each sequin is stitched to the cover with matching thread, and one tiny glass bead is stitched to the centre of the sequins at the same time.

Yet another method of making fabric-covered lampshades is shown in Fig. 27, and this method is one usually adopted by professional lampshade makers when covering shades with many curves and panels, and for large standard shades where it is difficult to keep the material tight while working large areas. It takes more time than the other methods described, and requires skilful handling to avoid making too many bulky seams, but if well done it produces a perfect shade.

Commence by inspecting the wire frame, as this is the basis of the finished work. It cannot be stressed too often that you cannot build a perfect cover on a frame which is not straight and free from rust marks. Bind the wires as has been described, taking care over the corners to avoid bulk. Cut a pattern for each

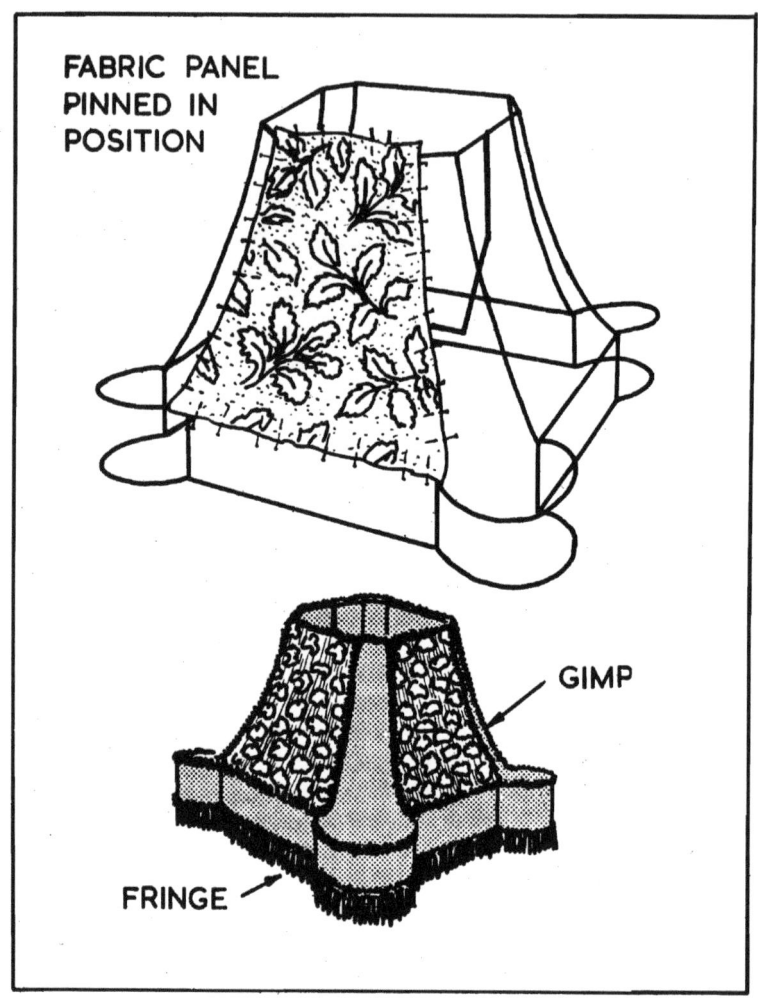

FIG. 27. METHOD OF DECORATING

separate panel of the frame and place the pattern pieces on the material, making quite sure that each piece is on the true bias of the material. Check this very carefully, as faults cannot be remedied once the material is cut—making a mistake in a large cover of a costly material could be a very expensive business. Cut the material to shape, allowing a good inch to an inch and a half all round each pattern piece.

Take one panel at a time and pin the material to the wires bordering the panel, as shown in Fig. 27. Pin at the top first, then the bottom, and finally at the side wires. Make absolutely certain that the material is quite taut and the strain evenly distributed in all directions, then cut off any surplus material along one edge to within about a quarter of an inch.

Using a thread of matching colour and a fairly fine sewing needle, stitch the material to the binding round the wire, turning the edge under with the needle and removing the pins one at a time until the panel has been completed. While stitching trim off the surplus material at each edge. Do not take a short cut and trim all the edges of a panel before commencing the stitching, as the material will fray when pulled taut.

Continue in this way, completing one panel at a time, until all the shade is covered. If the work is neatly done there should be no raw edges visible from the inside of the shade, but if the material is thin or of a dark colour and a lining, perhaps in pale pink, is wanted, it can be made in exactly the same way and sewn in from the inside of the frame. This should be done first before the covering material is stitched on. These shades are decorated in any of the ways described in the chapter on decorating lampshades at the end of the book. The one illustrated has the seams covered with fancy gimp, and a fringe hangs from the lower wire. Stitch the fringe under the lower wire, then stitch the gimp over the wire.

Besides these orthodox methods of covering shades with fabrics there are several novelty ways in which attractive shades may be made. One of these is to use thin material, lace or net, over a stiff paper. Fig. 28 illustrates a table-lamp shade that is very effective and very simple to make. Two lampshade-frame rings of the same size are required, and 8-in. rings were used for the one shown. The bottom ring should have a gimbal fitting. The top ring (without the gimbal) should be bound all round with bias binding and the second ring (with the gimbal) should be bound with the exception of the gimbal. Make a circular pattern to cover the top ring, cut this out in stiff white drawing paper and stitch the circle of paper to the ring. This must be done carefully or the paper may tear. Now cut a strip of paper about 6 in. wide and the length of the circumference of the ring plus ½ in. for the seam. Gum the strip of paper into a tube and when dry stitch one end of this tube to the ring which is covered with paper.

c

FIG. 28. LACE AND PAPER SHADE

Stitch the other end of the paper tube to the second ring. This paper base should now be covered with net. Cut a double circle of net for the top and pleat strips of net round the shade, stitching them neatly into place on the rings.

One-and-a-half-inch ribbon is used for the trimming. Make a ruching of the ribbon and stitch over the top seam, then gather the ribbon to a frill and stitch round the bottom of the frame. Make several small rosettes of the net and stitch them to the centre of the top of the shade, or one or two very tiny artificial flowers could be placed in the centre to finish the shade. However, do not use too much decoration, as the whole point of this type of shade is its daintiness. Many ideas will occur to the handicraft worker which can be carried out in this way, combining paper and fabric. For example, a lampshade to resemble a drum could very easily be made to use in a small boy's room.

CHAPTER VIII

Stiff lampshade covers: Paper shades — pleated lampshade — pie-frill lampshade covers — "Coolie Hat" type of cover — fluted shade in buckram — velvet and parchment shade.

BUCKRAM and paper are two very useful materials for covering lampshades, as they can be used either separately or combined with other materials which require stiffening. Both can be decorated by painting in various ways or by attaching motifs in felt or coloured paper to them. Paper lampshades are particularly useful where a long-lasting shade is not required. They are attractive in appearance, and being inexpensive may be changed frequently when soiled.

Paper lends itself easily to pleating and folding. Good-quality cartridge paper should be used for the covers, and before commencing a shade the pleating should be practised on some oddments of stiff paper, as once it is creased the paper cannot be uncreased. It is therefore necessary to be very sure where the pleats are to be formed before commencing a shade.

The first shade described is shown in Fig. 29A. It is a simple, straight pleated paper shade. This style is most suitable for large standard shades, but it may also be used to cover a pendant or table lamp. A pleated cover of this kind requires an "Empire" shape foundation frame which need not have side members, as the paper will be stiff enough to hold the rings in position. Commence by inspecting the wire rings and then binding them with bias tape, or painting the wires in a colour which will tone with the paper cover.

The width of the paper for the cover should be the depth of the frame plus about 2 in., to overhang the edges of the frame at top and bottom; the length of the paper should be three times the circumference of the ring at the bottom of the shade. The paper can be joined to obtain the necessary length, if the pieces are pleated first, then joined as shown in Fig. 29A. The pleats may be any size, but normally they are about 1 in. wide when used for an average-sized frame.

Lightly mark the position of each pleat on the edges of the paper with a pencil. The folding must be done with great care, and a piece of thin smooth wood a little longer than the width of the paper will be a great help in folding the pleats. Place the

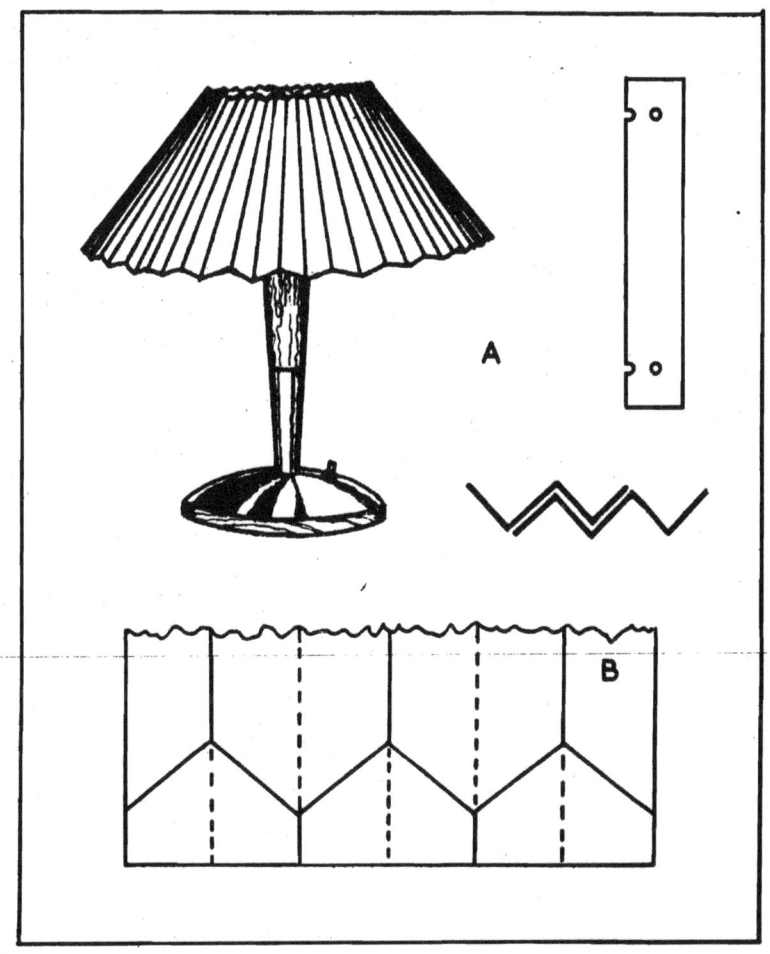

FIG. 29. PLEATING PAPER COVERS

length of paper on the edge of a flat surface and place the strip of wood under the paper, with an edge level with the pencil marks, and press the paper down to obtain a neat fold. The paper will need to be worked backwards and forwards several times to make a good fold.

After all the paper has been pleated, holes must be punched through the centre of the pleats about 1 in. from either end, and the holes should be large enough to allow a silk cord to be threaded through them. Small nicks should next be cut in the inside fold of the pleats, just below the punched holes—these nicks are required to hold the pleated cover to the rings of the frame. The cord should be inserted through the large holes. With this done, place the cover over the frame and draw the cords up tightly without crushing the paper; place the pleats evenly round the frame before tying the ends of the cords. The spacing of the holes and the nicks is shown in Fig. 29.

A very pretty variation of these pleated shades is obtained by using coloured "Cellophane" over cartridge paper. Make up a plain "Empire" shape cover in cartridge paper and stitch it to a wire frame, then pleat the "Cellophane" on to the paper shade, sticking each pleat top and bottom with transparent "Cellophane" tape. A narrow gimp or velvet ribbon can then be stitched over the tape to finish the cover.

Pie-frill lampshade covers in pleated paper have been introduced to this country from Scandinavia and have become very popular. The material required for a pie-frill shade should be about three times the required length of pleated cover, and the width should be the height of the frame plus an overlap of 2 in. or 3 in. top and bottom. The piece of paper for the cover should be lightly marked in pencil for 1-in. pleats, following the diagram in Fig. 29 for the markings. Mark the paper very lightly with pencil, so that the marks can later be removed with a soft rubber.

After marking the pleat lines the guide lines for the frills must be marked. In this shade the frill turns under at the top and the bottom of the cover, but many variations of this can be worked. Next the short crease lines should be marked from the guide lines (see Fig. 29B). It is most important to appreciate that some of the pleats fold outwards and some of them fold inwards. To clarify this, the diagram shows those that fold out by a continuous line, and those which fold in by a series of dashes.

With all the crease lines marked, the cover should be scored. Do this with a blunt tool guided by a straight-edge, and keep the pressure even. The next part of the work consists of folding, and this is best done on a smooth flat surface. If the scoring has been done properly the paper should fold easily without cracking. Fold each pleat and turning separately; it is not very easy to turn a well-shaped pleat at first, and some practice may be required. Do not crease all the pleats first and then the turnings, thinking to make things easier, or you may become confused with the "unders" and "overs." Work slowly and methodically until all the cover has been pleated. The ends will need to be overlapped and glued to hold them firmly.

The next step in the work is to mount the cover on the frame, and there are two ways in which this can be done. The cover may be stitched to the tape of the bound frame at the points where the turned-in folds touch the frame—if this course is adopted care must be taken to space the pleats evenly—or the cover may be joined to the frame by punching small holes through each inner fold, where it will meet the frame. Diagonal slits are then made from the holes to the edges, so that the frame wire can be slipped through these cuts to rest in the holes.

The simplest shape of all to make in paper is the "Coolie Hat" type of cover, and this style of frame is very popular in France, where they are often used three or four in a room, each one tinted a different colour. For this only one foundation ring is required, and this must include the gimbal fitting. For a pendant shade the point of the hat hangs downwards, while for a reading lamp it points upwards.

To make the "Coolie Hat" shade cover, cut a circle of paper with the diameter of the circle measuring about 2 in. to 3 in. larger than the diameter of the wire ring. Cut a line from the outer edge to the centre of the paper, then start stitching it to the wire ring, which should previously have been bound with bias binding. Continue stitching around the ring until the paper meets and cut away the surplus wedge of paper, allowing a margin for gumming the two edges together. It will be found that, as progress is made round the wire frame with the stitching, the shape will form itself. The depth of the cone can be altered; its size depends upon how much larger than the diameter of the wire ring the paper circle is cut.

A wide gimp should then be stitched over the join to the point of the "Coolie Hat" and back down the other side. Gimp should also be attached over the wire edge. If a hanging lamp is required, make the "coolie hat" shape with a plain wire ring without a gimbal, and attach cords to the edges by which it may be hung from the ceiling.

Buckram is one of the most useful materials for making lampshades, and is obtainable in white. It has an attractive appearance and can be tinted any shade quite easily by brushing over with water colour, though care must be taken not to make the material too damp, as this will make the buckram lose its stiffness; or it can be decorated by any of the painting methods; alternatively it can have designs, cut from other materials, stuck to it.

A very simple flared shade in buckram is illustrated in Fig. 30. To make this you will require two wire rings and some buckram. Bind the rings with bias binding as has been previously described, then cut a circle of buckram having a diameter twice that of the bottom ring, and cut a circle the same size as the smaller ring from the centre of the buckram. Bind round the edges of the buckram circle with bias binding and stitch the buckram to the top ring, using matching cotton. Pin the lower edge of the buck-

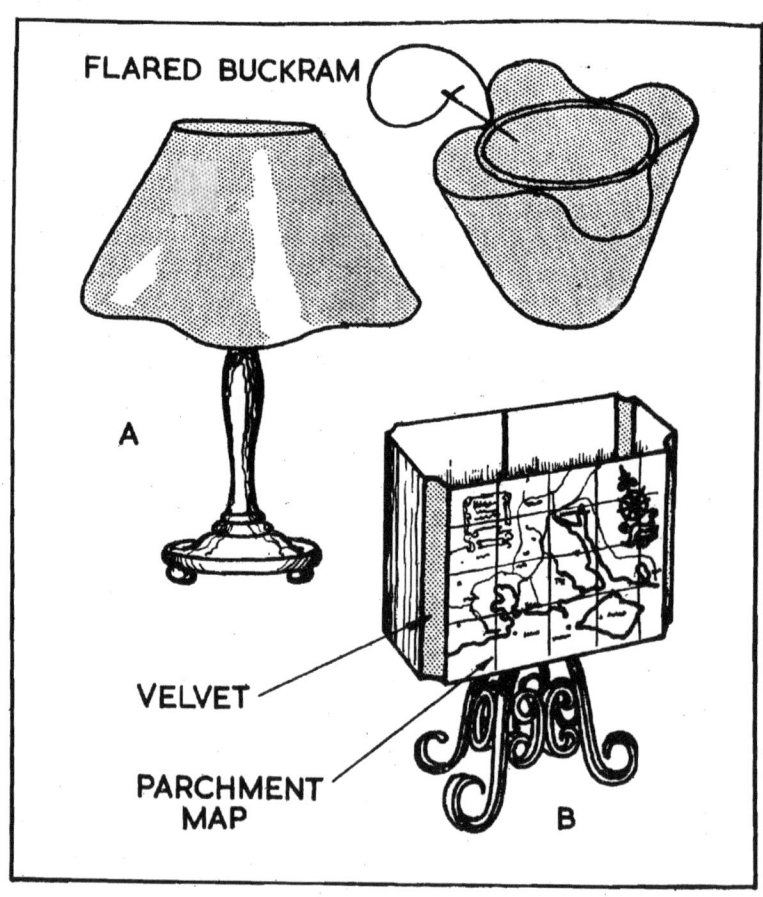

FIG. 30. FLARED SHADE

ram to the lower ring of the frame in wide flares, making sure the flares are all equally spaced, and stitch them to the frame where the buckram touches the ring. If a more decorative shade is required, stitch or gum the gimp round the edges of the frame.

It is often decided that a lampshade to match the curtains or covers in a room would be a good idea, and then the idea is dropped because of the difficulty of using the material as a lampshade covering. This is where buckram can be put to good use, especially when a very soft material is to be used as a cover. The buckram serves the dual purpose of a lining and a stiffening.

Inspect the foundation frame and bind it with bias binding. Next make a very accurate pattern and cut it out in the buckram. After cutting out the buckram, wipe over each piece with a damp sponge. There is no necessity to use a lot of water, use just enough to soften the glue in the buckram. Place the covering material over the buckram shapes, right side of the material facing you, and then place a damp cloth over it, then iron with a hot iron. The stiffening in the buckram softens and the material sticks to the buckram; for this reason it is necessary to use as hot an iron as the material will take without damaging it. It will be necessary to test the iron on some spare pieces before commencing, so as to obtain the right heat. When the material has been ironed on to the buckram leave it until it has cooled, then trim round the buckram shapes and make the cover in the usual way. When using patterned material for a panelled shade, make certain that the pattern runs the same way on all the panels, and if the pattern is large, that it is nicely centred on each pattern.

There is no necessity to cover all the shade with material; in some cases a pleasing effect can be obtained by cutting out the pattern motifs and sticking them on the buckram. Coloured laces or nets make very lovely shades if used over buckram in this way.

It is also possible to make many novelty shades by cutting out the shapes in buckram. A buckram shade can be decorated with gimp and fringe. In this case it is best to stick the decoration to the shade, using a white handicraft adhesive. Use only a small amount of the adhesive—if too much is used it will soak through the gimp and cause ugly stains. Buckram and velvet go together very well, and a plain buckram shade decorated with velvet bow, or with a velvet ribbon ruched around the edges, looks very effective. Buckram is easily tinted to any required colour. Use a large brush and brush over with water colour or fabric dye. Keep as dry as possible while working and leave to dry thoroughly before making up.

Velvet by itself, though a very lovely material, is not entirely suitable for lampshade making, as it is not sufficiently translucent to allow the light through, and secondly it has too "heavy" an appearance. However, velvet can be used to great advantage with other materials. The most usual combination is velvet and parchment. In describing this type of shade, real parchment is meant—not the imitation paper parchment, but parchment which is usually obtainable in the form of old maps, deeds, etc. The velvet is used only in small panels, to offset with its rich colour the creaminess of the parchment. This type of shade is suitable for dining rooms or lounges.

The shade illustrated in Fig. 30B is an oblong one and the four small corner panels are covered with velvet. This shape is very suitable for a reading lamp which is to stand on a table or against a wall.

These parchment maps and deeds, being very old, often require cleaning before being made into lampshades, and it is first necessary to find out if the writing on them is fast. To do this, test it in the following way. Wet a small part of the ink and cover the part with blotting paper; rub over the blotting paper with the unsharpened end of a pencil. Remove the blotting paper, and if it is unmarked the writing will withstand careful cleaning.

To clean the parchment mix a very weak solution of oxalic acid in water and wash the parchment with this. Use a sponge and work gently and quickly, and as soon as the parchment is clean, dry it with blotting paper. If the parchment deeds and maps are very old, and have creases and wrinkles in them, they will need a more thorough treatment to remove the fold creases; this treatment consists of re-backing the parchment, and is fully described in the book *Lampshade Making*[1] in the Foyles handbook series.

After cleaning and preparing the parchment, inspect and bind the frame. Then proceed to cover the narrow corner panels with velvet. Choose a rich dark colour—green or deep red are both good. Cut a strip of the material and place it over one of the corners. Pin the velvet to the binding at top and bottom edges of the frame, then pin the side of the strip of velvet to the side wires. Continue working in the manner described for fabric shades,

---

[1] *Lampshade Making*, by F. J. Christopher (Foyles, 2s. 6d.).

work round the corner piece, and, removing the pins one at a time, tighten the material and replace the pins. As these small panels are concave, the greatest stretch of the material must be down the length of the panel, so that the shape is maintained. Trim off any surplus material round the panel, leaving just enough to turn under. With a needle and suitably coloured thread stitch the panel to the binding on the wires. Fasten off securely and cover the other three corners in the same way.

Cut patterns for the two sides and two end panels in thin card, making quite certain that they are accurate. Position the panels on the parchment and mark and cut it to shape. The parchment is stitched to the frame, and as these old maps, etc., are often rather brittle, it is best to pierce stitch holes first, using a fine bradawl. Care must be taken not to break the material at the edges. Use a medium-sized needle and strong cotton and sew firmly, but on no account pull the cotton too tightly or it may cut the parchment. It is a great help to use clothes pegs or paper clips to hold the panel in position when stitching it.

For decorating the edges choose a simple gimp or braid to match the velvet, remembering that the velvet and old parchment have great beauty in themselves, and the purpose of the gimp is not really to "decorate" the shade but to neaten the edges and to complement the mellowed colouring of the parchment. If a fringe is required, choose one of the antique styles with a bobble edge rather than the straight rayon ones, which are more suitable for use with plastic materials.

CHAPTER IX

Basketry lampshades: Lampshade for a reading lamp — materials — method of weaving the shade — constructing the base — finishing — wiring the lampholder.

DURING the past few years woven basketry furniture has again become popular, and the idea of using basketry materials has now spread to lampshade making. It is little wonder that these basketry lampshades have become so popular. They are inexpensive to make, and look right in any but the most conventionally furnished rooms; also, these shades are practically indestructible, and can even be scrubbed with soap and water over and over again.

In Fig. 31 is illustrated a woven lampshade on a reading lamp the base of which is also basketry, and which is woven over an empty jar. Any kitchen will provide suitable jars for base foundations; empty pickle or honey jars are best, but any reasonably heavy bottle or jar will do.

Most basketry lampshades are made after the "Empire" shape, but it is possible to introduce considerable variety by means of various styles in edgings, by trimming in coloured raffia, or by introducing coloured wooden beads into the borders.

To make the shade shown in the illustration you will require a small wire ring containing a gimbal, a quantity of No. 3 cane for weaving (a pound by weight should be more than ample) and enough No. 6 cane to cut twenty-seven stakes 18 in. in length. The shade is worked on a cardboard base in the same way as one works cane on a wooden base, and when the shade is completed the cardboard is torn away.

To commence the basketry lampshade, cut out a circle of cardboard a little larger than the wire ring; place the wire ring on the cardboard circle and pencil round the outline of the wire. On this pencil line punch twenty-seven holes at equal distances apart, large enough to take the No. 6 cane. Soak the cane in water. Insert the 18-in. stakes into the holes and pull them through until they are about 4 in. above the cardboard. Tie the ends together on top of the cardboard, to keep them in position while the cover is being woven.

Soak the No. 3 cane in water to make it pliable, and work

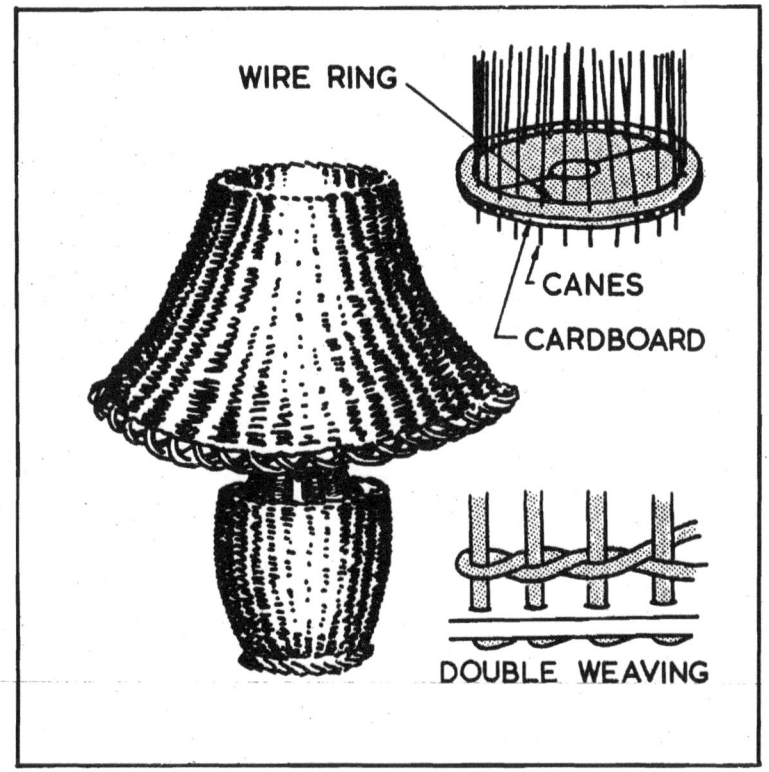

FIG. 31. BASKETRY SHADE AND BASE

about 2 in. of basketry in single weaving, then proceed in double weaving, shaping the shade outwards all the time. Directions for working the single and double weaving can only be given briefly here, and the worker who intends to make any quantity of these shades is advised to study *Basketry*,[1] a companion volume in the Foyles handbook series.

Single weaving consists of taking the weaving cane in front of one stake and behind the next stake, all round the base, while double weaving consists of bending the weaving cane in two, crossing the two ends, and slipping the loop thus formed over the first stake, continuing to weave as shown in Fig. 31. Continue in double weaving, keeping the stakes bent outwards in a graceful

[1] *Basketry*, by F. J. Christopher (Foyles, 2s. 6d.).

curve until the shade is about 6 in. to 7 in. deep. Before commencing the border, soak the stakes for about fifteen minutes in hot water so that they bend easily. Proceed by bending each stake down behind one, in front of two, behind one, in front of two, behind one, thus leaving the ends of the stakes inside the work. The worker with a knowledge of basketry can work many fancy openwork edges in place of this simple one.

Untie the bottom stakes and work the top of the shade. Place the wire ring on the cardboard, with alternate stakes inside and outside the ring; this is shown in the illustration Fig. 31. Work the border in the same way as the bottom edge. Bend down a stake and pass it behind two, in front of one, and behind the next one, all the way round, so that the ends are inside the shade. Leave until the stakes are quite dry again, then clip off the ends near to the basket work, and tear away the cardboard to complete the shade. Should the basketry lampshade seem out of shape when it is finished, it can be improved by soaking in hot water for a few minutes and then bending to a better shape.

The base of the lamp illustrated is made from a stone 4-lb. jam jar. A metal batten holder was purchased and bolted to the metal lid of the one shown, to hold the bulb and flex. To make the basketry cover for the jar, first wash and thoroughly dry the jar, then make a base to fit the bottom of the jar. This may either be cut out in plywood or in thick cardboard. Several thicknesses of card can be glued together until the right thickness is obtained. Make the base about $\frac{1}{4}$ in. larger all round than the base of the bottle, punch an uneven number of holes round the base $\frac{1}{4}$ in. in from the edge, and cut a stake of No. 6 cane for each hole about 6 in. longer than the height of the jar. Soak the cane and push each stake through the holes until about 3 in. protrudes. Tie the long ends of the stakes together, dampen the short ends, and work them to make a border under the base as follows. Bend down a stake, pass it behind two stakes, in front of the next stake, and behind the next stake; repeat this all round the base so that the points of the stakes are inside the work. Later, when the cane has dried, the ends can be trimmed off close to the edge of the work.

Untie the top stakes, and using soaked No. 5 cane and single weaving, work one or two rounds over and under the stakes. Place the jar or bottle inside the stakes. Continue weaving, keeping the basketry pulled tightly to the sides of the jar, so that it takes the exact shape of the jar. When the top is reached, finish with the same border as the base—that is, bend one stake behind two stakes, in front of one stake, behind one stake, only this time finish so that the ends are on the outside and the basketry is pulled tightly to the top of the lampstand. Leave till the canes have dried completely, then clip off the ends. The lampholder should be wired in the usual way and the flex may be tucked away inside the basketry cover of the base.

CHAPTER X

Table lamp bases: Converting bottles and jars — fitting a lamp socket and switch — "Pifco" adaptor — use of a back-plate — drilling a hole for the flex — suitable drills — precautions.

MANY of the lampshades described in this book are suitable for use as covers for table lamps, and in addition to making attractive lampshades, the home handicraft worker can make many very effective bases for table lamps. A wide variety of ordinary articles can quite simply be transformed into table lamps, and some suggestions are given in Fig. 32.

Bottles and jars are favourites for conversion to table-lamp

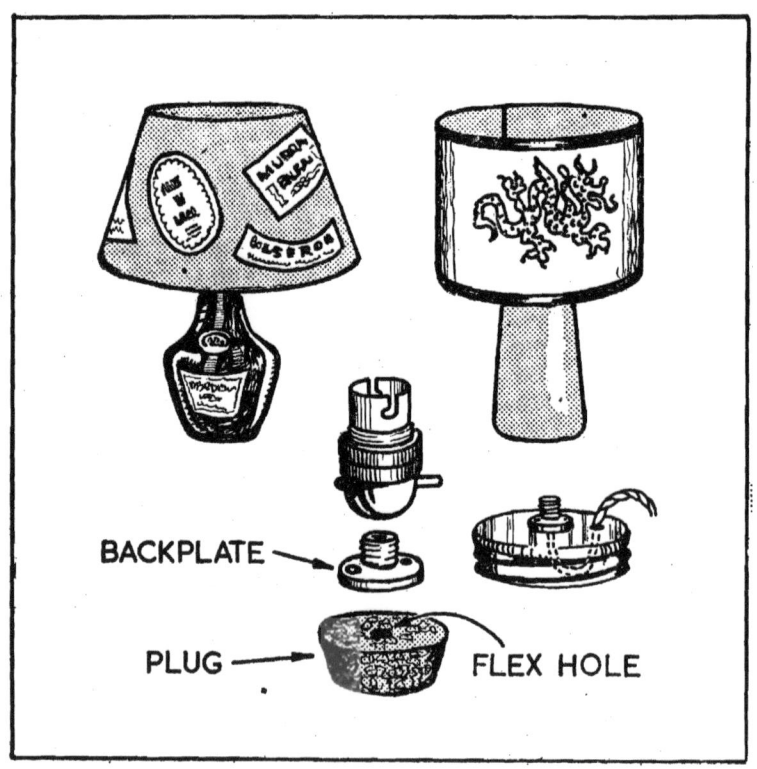

FIG. 32. TABLE-LAMPS

bases, and other articles that may be used for this purpose include vases, candlesticks, large polished pieces of wood, and various kinds of ornaments. In most cases converting any article to a lamp base consists in fitting the object with a lamp socket and switch so that it may easily and efficiently be wired for electric current.

Converting jars and bottles, vases and ornaments with lids or necks is a fairly simple matter. This can be done by using a special adaptor made for this purpose. This is the "Pifco" adaptor, which consists of a socket to take the electric bulb and switch together as one unit, that is secured to a cork. The cork is fashioned as a roll which may be adjusted to fit most bottles with no neck. If this type of fitting is used for converting a bottle into a lampshade base, it will be necessary to make provision for fitting the flex which is attached to the lampholder through a central hole in the cork stopper. For this it will be necessary to drill a hole in the glass, and this is described later in this chapter.

Wine bottles make very attractive lamp bases, and the design motif may be emphasized by attaching labels from wine bottles to the shade, if it has a smooth cover. Parchment lends itself extremely well to this type of cover, and the labels and cover should be given a coat of clear varnish so that they may easily be cleaned without damage.

A method of fitting wide-necked jars and bottles with a lamp-holder socket is by using what is known as a back-plate. This is illustrated in Fig. 32. The back-plate may be soldered or bolted to a metal jar cover or closure of wood or cork that has been cut to shape to fit the top of a bottle or jar. The back-plate may be screwed into the main material. If a back-plate is used the lamp socket must be of the type which is fitted with an internal thread which screws over the threaded base of the back-plate. In the case of a wide-necked jar or bottle the flex hole may be made in a closure as illustrated in Fig. 32, and the socket may be of the type fitted with a switch, or a separate "torpedo" switch may be fitted to the flex. For this type of lamp base a batten-holder type of lamp socket may be successfully used in place of the back-plate and holder.

The batten holder is attached to the closure of the jar, which may be cork, wood, or a metal lid, by bolting or screwing it in place, and if a batten holder is used it will also be necessary to make provision for the entry of the flex, so that it may be attached to the connections of the lampholder.

If the flex is to run through the lamp base it will be necessary to make a hole for this purpose. If the base is wood it will be found a simple matter to drill a hole for the flex, but if the table-lamp base is of glass, stoneware or china, it will not be quite so easy to make the necessary hole. In most towns this can be done locally by taking the base with the position of the hole marked to a hardware merchant or builders' merchant, who will very often drill glass and china at the owner's risk.

The drilling may also be done by the lampshade maker, and for this purpose special drill bits may be obtained. These may be used with the electrically powered drills or with hand drills. These special drills with hardened points are normally used for drilling holes in brick, stone, tile, marble, cement or slate, and although they are not specially manufactured for drilling glass or china-ware, they may be successfully used provided reasonable care is taken while the work is being done. In this work it is essential to ensure that a firm and even pressure is maintained while the drill is being rotated against the material.

It will be found necessary to mark the point of entry in the material to be drilled, and this can be done with the tang of a file. It is necessary to make only a very small indentation, so that the point of the drill is guided and does not "wander" as the drill is rotated.

Full details of the use of carbon-tipped drills, which are manufactured under various trade names, may be obtained from the suppliers, and the drills are available in a very large range of sizes. For the flex of most types of lamp a $\frac{1}{4}$-in. drill will be found a suitable size.

During the drilling of glass or chinaware it is advisable to use a lubricant to prevent the tool and material from becoming overheated. A suitable lubricant for this purpose can be made by dissolving crushed camphor in turpentine. During the work of drilling it is important to ensure that the drill is pressed firmly into the hole being cut as the drill is rotated, and the direction of the drill should not be changed. If this is done the glass or china-ware will in all probability crack or split.

Care must be taken in wiring the lamp base to ensure that the connections are properly made. The covering of the flex should not be frayed, and connections both to the adaptor and the plug should be made so that the ends of the wire are securely held and sufficient insulation is provided to prevent the two wires of the flex from touching. If the worker has no knowledge at all of electrical wiring it is advised that this be done by a competent electrician.

CHAPTER XI

Decorating lampshades: Tinting — painted designs — transfers — coloured paper shapes — floral motifs — repeating design — wax crayon designs — fringes and braids — lace decoration — "shadow" work — gathered or pleated frills — ruching — shell edging — Toby frills — knitted fringe.

A WELL-MADE lampshade does not require much in the way of decoration, as most of the materials used have their own beauty. However, many lampshades may require some embellishment, used discreetly. Much depends upon the purpose of the shade and the general furnishing and colour scheme of the room in which the shade is used.

Parchment, vellum and stiff paper shades are often improved by tinting the inside of the covers with a warm soft pink or yellow, and, being very plain in themselves, these materials make a perfect background for many forms of decoration. As a rule these shades do not appear at their best sporting large velvet bows or fabric ruchings, but they do look good with a painted design or decorative stuck-on labels, or even a carefully executed design built up of coloured paper shapes. Alternatively, a wide variety of coloured transfers can be purchased, and these are ideal for use on parchment.

Decorating can be carried out before the shade is made up, but in some cases it will be found easier to do the decorating after making the shade, and, unless you are an artist, you will find it necessary to trace the design on to the parchment or paper before making up the shade.

Designs may be traced very easily on to parchment or vellum, because of its translucency. Draw or trace the design on a piece of white paper (do not use a ball-point pen for this, as the ink may rub off) and place the drawn design under the vellum. Then lightly pencil in the outlines of the design, which will clearly be seen through the parchment. Fig. 33 shows several decorative designs which are made up from the type of transfers easily obtained from handicraft dealers or stationers.

In all branches of handicrafts there are craftworkers who spoil a well-made and finely designed piece of work by either over-decoration or insufficient finishing. A good finish is very necessary to lampshade making, and as this is one of the crafts in which you

FIG. 33. TRANSFERS

can "see it growing" the finishing processes should not be unduly hurried. The good craftsman does not try to hide inferior work with decoration. Braids and fringes will not hide blemishes or inadequately finished lampshades.

It is not necessary to be an artist to be able to put a satisfactory finishing touch to a lampshade. It is largely a matter of using suitable materials and practice in applying the various types of decoration, although it is also largely a matter of personal taste. Obviously it is only common sense for the worker who wishes to sell the goods produced to bear in mind the modern trend of simplicity in line and form and the avoidance of over-decoration.

Quick and attractive décor results can be obtained by using coloured paper shapes on parchment or vellum lampshades. These very colourful shapes may be purchased in boxes of assorted shapes for a few pence and, being ready gummed, take only a few moments to put into place. They can be made up into an endless variety of amusing and attractive "repeat" designs. If the worker has plenty of time to put into the project, there is great scope in making wall friezes to match the lampshades. Many suitable motifs may be devised for decorating the walls and lampshades for shops, nurseries, kitchens and bathrooms.

Some suitable designs are shown in Fig. 33. It should of course be the craftworker's aim to produce original designs, but those without any great artistic ability will find a wealth of ideas in embroidery transfers. Often it is possible to combine parts of two or three transfers to produce a really interesting design.

Small circles about the size of a sixpence may be used to great advantage. For instance, a plain "Empire" style frame can be covered with a creamy-coloured parchment, with the top and bottom of the shade bound with a deep blue *passe partout*, then blue circles of paper can be stuck at intervals all over the shade; or a pale rose-coloured sheepskin parchment with silver trimmings may be worked. There are endless variations of colour schemes for this treatment. Another idea can be worked by attaching small circles of paper in many colours, overlapping each other all round the top and bottom of a shade.

On panelled shades, floral motifs make lovely corner decorations, but care must be taken not to over-elaborate the decorating of lampshades, and it is not necessary to place a motif in every panel. Floral designs are easy to work and have the advantage of fitting into almost any colour scheme. A spray of flowers will introduce ample colour if the lampshade covering is plain— motifs made up from bell-shaped flowers, sprays of blossom or autumn leaves are all very attractive and colourful. When making these motifs there is no need to cut each piece separately to shape; the various shapes may be selected from the boxes of mixed paper shapes obtainable or, if preferred, they may be cut from strips of gummed paper. The design must be worked out in colour, then the various parts traced on to thin card, and the card cut out and used as a pattern. Several thicknesses of gummed paper can be cut at the same time with sharp scissors.

If a repeating design is being used, a strip of paper can be bent as shown in Fig. 34. After folding, the motif design should be traced on to the paper and all the folds cut through together. Remember that parts of the side lines of the paper must not be cut to result in a long shaped strip. Choose a simple pattern for

FIG. 34. REPEATING DECORATIVE DESIGNS

the first attempt, and practise on some strips of newspaper first.

If any difficulty is experienced in making the paper shapes stick to the parchment, wipe over the area to be decorated with "Thawpit," which will remove the grease from the parchment. To finish, when all the design is stuck on, coat the shade with clear varnish.

There are two main ways in which a fabric-covered shade may be decorated. The fabric itself may be decorated, or trimmings may be added by using gimps, braids, fringes, etc. In most cases it will be found best to paint or dye the fabric before making up the cover.

Perhaps the simplest way of doing this is with children's ordinary wax crayons. When fixed, these colours are quite fast to light, and if necessary may be washed and ironed. This method is a very inexpensive way of producing the most luxurious-looking hand-coloured shades. For a few pence one can buy a packet of these crayons. Almost any smooth material which can be ironed with a fairly warm iron is suitable for this type of decoration, but washing satin is widely used for lampshade covering and is particularly good.

In most cases it will be necessary to decorate the material before covering the shade. Have ready an iron and a table or other flat surface on which you can iron. Decide on a suitable design—a small motif as shown in Fig. 34 can be scattered all over the material and makes a good design for practising, but if you feel that free-hand drawing is beyond you, embroidery transfers are very useful for obtaining design shapes. If the material is transparent, slip the design underneath the material and colour on the top of it. If using embroidery transfers, try to choose a yellow one, so that the outlines will not mark the material too much.

Having transferred the design outlines on the material, the next stage is to commence the colouring with the crayons. Place a large sheet of blotting paper on the table. Pin the material on top of the blotting paper, with the right side of the material uppermost. The blotting paper should have previously been heated by ironing it, and the iron should be kept hot while the work is in progress, so that the blotting paper can be re-ironed at intervals to keep it warm. A little practice will soon indicate how hot the paper should be. If it is too cool, it will not draw the crayon colours through the material, but if it is too hot it will melt the crayon too quickly and the colours will run. One colour may be used on top of another for shading—in fact, the colouring is done exactly as if the picture were being crayoned on paper. When all the colouring has been done, it is necessary to fix the colour—and this is done by placing a piece of blotting paper on top and beneath the work, and ironing over the top of the pile.

It is possible to buy a great variety of fringes and braids for decorating lampshades, but some of them are rather expensive. The craftworker will often find that a more attractive finish can be obtained by making one's own frills and ruches, especially for the more luxurious type of shade.

A peach silk shade of simple shape for a bedroom may be improved by two or three rows of black or coffee-coloured lace round top and bottom, as shown in Fig. 35. First pull the drawing thread which is woven in the straight edge of the net or lace to gather it, and attach the frill either by stitching with whipping stitch or sticking it to the cover with one of the white handicraft adhesives. Small lace motifs attached to a silk shade give it a very pleasing effect when the lamp is lit. A white buckram shade can be completely covered with black or coloured lace, and this is easily done. The cover should be cut out in buckram and covered with a piece of lace, and ironed with a fairly hot iron over a damp cloth—this will cause the stiffening in the buckram to soften and hold the lace in place. Leave the cover for a short time to allow the stiffening to harden, then make up the shade in the usual way.

Another very attractive method of decorating a plain buckram shade is by "shadow" work. To do this a piece of georgette or other sheer material to cover the buckram is required, also some scraps of material in a deeper shade and some embroidery silk. First mark out a small, simple floral design on the georgette, and work the leaves and stems very neatly in back-stitch so that there are no visible joins or knots. Cut the small pieces of material to roughly the shapes of the flowers and place them between the buckram and georgette, so that they show through under the flowers in the design. Iron the buckram and georgette, protecting the materials with a damp cloth, then make up the shade in the usual way. When lit the effect will be of shadowy flowers showing through the cover.

Simple gathered frills or pleated frills and various types of ruching all make most decorative edges for fabric-covered lampshades. Fig. 35 shows five types of inexpensive edgings which can be really glamorous. Fig. 35A is a straight gathered frill of the same material as the shade itself. For this style cut a straight strip of material about $\frac{1}{2}$ in. wider than the finished frill is to be, and approximately one and a half times to twice the required length. Neaten one long edge with a narrow hem, the other long edge is turned over about $\frac{1}{4}$ in. and pressed. Run a gathering thread through this edge, dip the frill in a solution of plastic starch, dry and iron it, then pull the gathering thread until the

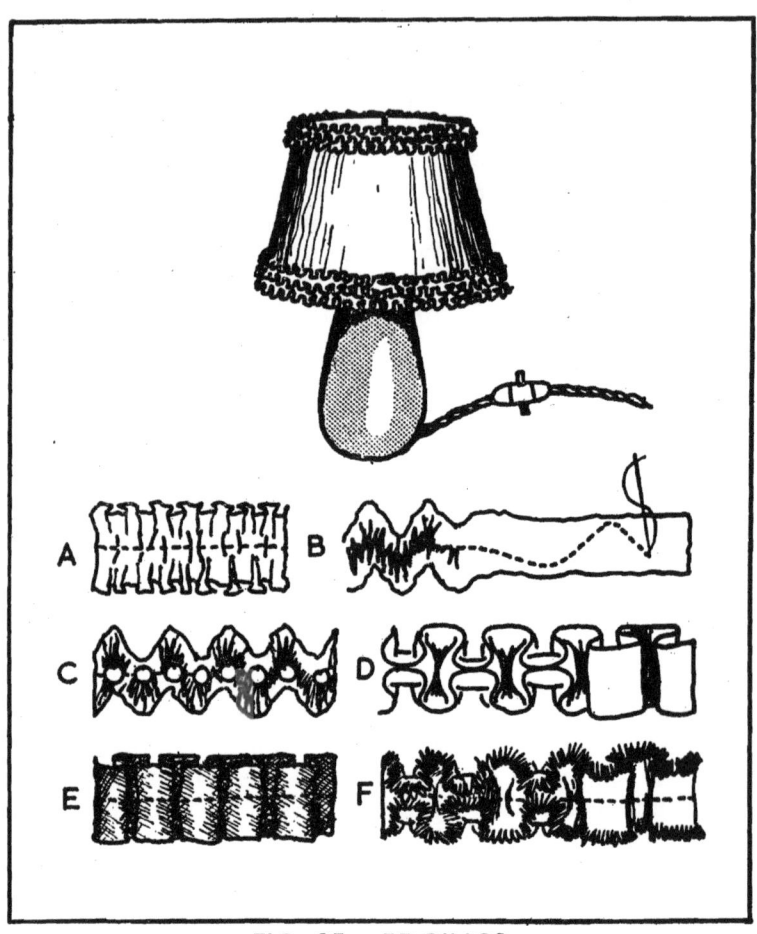

FIG. 35. EDGINGS

frill is the required length, then lightly stitch to edge of frame with matching thread.

Fig. 35B shows a shell gathering which makes an attractive edge. For this a length of material about 2 in. wide is required, or if ribbon is used it should be about 1 in. wide and at least twice as long as the finished length is to be.

If strips of the lampshade covering material are being used, turn both edges of each strip over on the wrong side and press well. Run a gathering thread along the folded material or ribbon, working the stitching zigzag up to the top edge and down to the bottom edge. Repeat the zigzag stitching keeping the points about 1 in. apart on each edge, and draw the gathering thread up until the zigzags form a straight line. This trimming may be lightly stitched to the edges of the shade, or it may be cemented to the cover with a colourless adhesive such as "Mystic." When using frills and ruchings as trimmings avoid handling them as much as possible, so that they keep their fresh, crisp appearance.

The finish in Fig. 35c is similar to shell edging, and it may be made in a contrasting material or with strips of the covering material. For a rather special trimming use gold or silver thread for the stitching and stitch a tiny pearl between each shell.

Commence by cutting strips, about $1\frac{1}{4}$ in. wide, on the cross of the material. Fold each over on the wrong side of the material and seam. Turn the tubes thus made the right side out with the help of a safety pin, as shown in the illustration. Press well so that the roll of material lies flat and smooth. Thread a longish needle with a double thread of sewing silk or stranded cotton, and pierce the strips to bring out the needle on the right side of the material (see the diagram). Put the needle vertically behind the roll and not through it, with the thread held under the needle, pull the needle through upwards and towards the worker and draw the thread very tight. Pass the needle along the inside of the roll, putting it in on the right side of the knot just made, and bring it out again about $\frac{1}{4}$ in. to $\frac{1}{2}$ in. away, depending upon the width of the roll.

In Fig. 35D is illustrated a very effective Toby frill. For use on lampshades this type of edging is usually made in velvet or taffeta ribbon. If other material is used, choose a very stiff one such as starched muslin or organdie. The strips for this type of frill are cut on the straight of the material and the strips of material are pinned into box pleats along each edge, then machined or back-stitched with matching thread through the middle of the pleats. To make a Toby frill, three times the length of the finished frill in material or ribbon is required. Lightly catch the top and bottom of each pleat together as shown in the illustration.

Net makes a very pretty frill, requiring two to three times the finished length of the edge being treated. Cut strips of net and gather or pleat them, then stitch along their centre. The frill illustrated in Fig. 35E shows the net box-pleated.

A slightly more elaborate type of ruching is the rose ruching shown in Fig. 35F. This is made by cutting strips of taffeta on the bias about $1\frac{1}{2}$ in. wide. The edges of the strips are then frayed to a depth of about $\frac{3}{16}$ in. on each edge. Box-pleat the strips, pinning the pleats at top and bottom, and with matching thread stitch through the centre of the strip, picking up the centre of each pleat and joining it to its neighbour, so that a circular rose is formed, as in the illustration.

Such a wide variety of fringes can be purchased at reasonable cost that it is not always necessary to make them, but when making a special shade you may be unable to obtain a fringe of just the right shade of colour. In these cases it is very simple to knit a fringe, which may be worked in either single or double cotton. Number 12 knitting needles are used and a strip of very thick card the depth of the required fringe is also required.

Begin by casting on seven stitches with the cotton, then proceed as follows:

First Row.—Insert the needle in the first stitch in the usual way, take the strip of card and hold it between the thumb and first finger of the left hand close up to the work. Pass the thread along the back and then up the front of the mesh, and round the point of the right-hand needle. Knit off the stitch, keeping it close to the card on which the fringe is wound. Knit the following stitch plain, then make one stitch, knit two together, make one, knit two together, knit one.

Next Row.—Slip the first stitch and knit six. Repeat these two rows alternately for the length required. When the card is covered with loops, those at one end can be slipped off to make room for more. A twist is given to the loops of the fringe by inserting a knitting needle in the loop and twisting tightly, then drawing the needle out.

Lampshade making is a craft of unlimited scope, and is one that can bring much pleasure by profitably occupying spare time. Many more ideas for novel and practical shades not mentioned in this book because of lack of space will occur to the lampshade maker, who with a little experience will be able to adapt them to his needs. There is a good market for the completed lampshades, provided they are well made and reasonably priced.

www.ingramcontent.com/pod-product-compliance
Ingram Content Group UK Ltd.
Pitfield, Milton Keynes, MK11 3LW, UK
UKHW041227200426
11947UKWH00034B/183